REBUILDING TRUST

A Couple's Guide to Healing After Betrayal

MATT AND LAURA BURTON

Becoming Well, LLC

REBUILDING TRUST

A Couple's Guide to Healing After Betrayal

Copyright © 2023 by Becoming Well, LLC

All rights reserved. No part of this book may be reproduced or transmitted in any form, or by any means, electronic or mechanical, including photocopying, recording, or by information storage or retrieval systems, without permission in writing from the copyright owner.

The views and opinions expressed in this book are those of the author, and do not necessarily reflect the official policy or position of Becoming Well, LLC

Published by Becoming Well, LLC

www.MyBecomingWell.com

Library of Congress Control Number
Paperback ISBN: 979-8-8689-2058-5
E-book ISBN: 979-8-8689-2373-9

Cover design by Monira

Printed in the United States of America

Table Of Contents

Acknowledgments .... **ix**
Authors' Note .... **xi**
Introduction .... **xiii**

PART 1
Intimacy Avoidance and Betrayal 1

PART 2
The Rebuilding Trust Pyramid 7

PART 3
Rebuilding Trust Pyramid Layer #1 15
Trust-Building Behaviors 17

PART 4
Preparing A Disclosure 25

PART 5
Trust-Building Behavior #2 35

PART 6
Trust-Building Behavior #3 43

PART 7
Asking Questions 51

PART 8
Final Thoughts on Trust-Building Behaviors 61

PART 9
Trust-Breaking Behavior #1 67

PART 10
The role of boundaries 75

PART 11
Trust-Breaking Behavior #2 ... 87

PART 12
Trust-Building Belief #1 ... 93
Trust-Building Belief #2 ... 96

PART 13
Trust-breaking belief #1 ... 101
Trust-breaking belief #2 ... 104
Trust Breaking Belief #3 ... 109
Trust Breaking Belief #4 ... 111

PART 14
Rebuilding Trust Pyramid Layer #2 ... 115

PART 15
Wounded Partner Pitfalls Pitfall #1 ... 125
Pitfall #2 ... 127
Pitfall #3 ... 128
Pitfall #4 ... 129
Pitfall #5 ... 131

PART 16
Wounding Partner Pitfalls ... 135

PART 17
Pitfalls As a Couple ... 145

PART 18
Recovery Plans ... 155

PART 19
Recovery Plan #4 ... 171

PART 20
Recovery Plan #5 179

PART 21
Recovery Plan #6 187

PART 22
Rebuilding Trust Pyramid Layer #3 191

PART 23
Relationship Consistency 205

PART 24
Rebuilding Trust Pyramid Layer #4 213

PART 25
The Importance of Cultivating Good Intimacy Habits ...221

Conclusion 229

References 231

Glossary 237

About the Authors 243

Acknowledgments

Behind this book stand numerous people who helped, encouraged, and ultimately believed in us and in this work. We want to thank our family, friends, fellow recovery coaches and counselors, as well as the many individuals and couple clients that have trusted us to guide them through some of the hardest times in their lives. It has been the ultimate privilege to witness the transformational breakthroughs that happened when they followed the process and did the work. Thank you all.

We would especially like to thank Heart to Heart Counseling Center in Colorado Springs for their dedication to couples struggling with similar issues, for excellent training, and supporting us along the way.

Matt and Laura

Authors' Note

Although the publisher and the authors have made every effort to ensure that the information in this book was correct at press time and while this publication is designed to provide accurate information in regard to the subject matter covered, the publisher and the author assume no responsibility for errors, inaccuracies, omissions, or any other inconsistencies herein and hereby disclaim any liability to any party for any loss, damage, or disruption caused by errors or omissions, whether such errors or omissions result from negligence, accident, or any other cause.

This publication is meant as a source of valuable information for the reader, however it is not meant as a substitute for direct expert assistance. If such level of assistance is required, the services of a competent professional should be sought.

Matt and Laura Burton

www.MyBecomingWell.com

Introduction

Even as we write this book, we realize that no one who doesn't work in the same field that we do truly wants to be in a place where they need to read it. If you are here, and are not a coach or counselor, we assume that you have been affected by infidelity in one way or another and are likely in a great deal of emotional pain. For that, we are truly sorry. Perhaps you are someone who has engaged in infidelity-related behavior and are trying to understand what you can do in order to help your partner heal. Or maybe you are someone who has found out about your partner's betrayal and are trying to find a way to put the pieces of your life back together. Whatever your circumstances, we want to welcome you and to tell you that we are truly sorry for what you are going through. We also want to say that we are happy you picked up this book because we believe that it contains the help that you need in order to begin to rebuild trust in your relationship. Although the tools and advice offered here are in no way meant to replace professional therapy or coaching, the methods we describe have brought success to many couples wishing to rebuild their relationship in the aftermath betrayal. If you are a coach or counselor reading this, we hope that the information contained in these pages will equip you with the knowledge you need to help your clients that are struggling to rebuild trust after betrayal.

We feel that it is important to note that we take a three-part approach when it comes to recovery from betrayal. For many couples, the sole focus after betrayal for one or both partners is on the survival of the relationship. We believe that betrayal recovery happens in three distinct areas: recovery for the wounding partner, recovery for the wounded partner, and recovery for the relationship. When the focus is solely on saving the relationship, partners often miss the individual work that they could be doing to increase their chances of success. A relationship is only strong if both parties in that relationship bring their best efforts to the table. It is not possible to have a healthy relationship if both parties neglect their own personal development. Neither is it possible to have a strong relationship when one partner does the majority of the heavy lifting while the other one neglects their responsibility to show up. The relationship will struggle if both partners are not 100% committed to doing whatever it takes to make it strong.

This book was written as a companion to the group and individual intensives that we offer. These intensives were designed to help couples struggling through the aftermath of betrayal. Our goal in writing this material was to give you a clear path to rebuilding trust. We think it is important to point out that, even though we provide a roadmap to trust in this book, we are not suggesting that trusting again after betrayal is simple in any way. The path to recovery is long and, many times, difficult. It is full of unexpected twists and turns that will need to be navigated successfully over time if trust is to be restored. In our experience, the bulk of the heavy lifting involved in rebuilding trust takes an average of two years. This process can be significantly lengthened by complicating factors such as intimacy avoidance and dribbling disclosure. The reason for this is that those issues, especially when combined with the wounding partner's reluctance to be 100% accountable and transparent moving forward, create an unsafe situation for the wounded partner. Without safety, trust cannot be rebuilt.

As you read through this book, you will likely notice that much of the emphasis is placed on what the wounding partner needs to change in order to facilitate the rebuilding trust process. This is intentional. Although we understand it takes two to make a relationship work, and that no partner in any given relationship is perfect, standard relationship counseling and coaching do not work for couples experiencing difficulties from betrayal. It is our firm belief that, until the actions of the wounding partner have been fully addressed and atoned for, it is inappropriate to address other issues within the relationship. Additionally, any coach or counselor who asks a wounded partner to take even partial ownership of a wounding partner's bad behavior only adds to the immense pain that the wounded partner is already experiencing. A person who coaches or counsels in this way may inadvertently be excusing and/or minimizing the effect that a wounding partner's choices have had on the relationship. This is devastating to the wounded partner. We have worked with countless wounded partners who have not only been damaged by this type of coaching and counseling but have actually experienced it as a secondary form of abuse.

Infidelity is a major problem in relationships today. A study conducted by MSNBC of 70,000 people found that 28% of male participants and 18% of female participants admitted to cheating on their spouses. (Weaver, 2007) Although this percentage may not seem large, if it is at all representative of the country's population, we can assume that, in any one given population, over 45 million men and almost 30 million women have cheated on their spouses in the United States alone—and that only accounts for the married ones. One study through the American Psychological Association showed that 20-40% of divorces in the U.S. can be attributed to infidelity and that 42% of these divorced individuals reported having more than one affair. (Christiansen, Marin, Atkins, 2014) Furthermore, studies have shown positive correlations between infidelity and marital stress, conflict, depression, and anxiety.

(Gordon, Baucom, 1999) Research shows that emotional affairs are far more common than sexual ones. A study of over 94,000 participants showed that 90% of female participants and 77% of male participants admitted to having an emotional affair at some point during their relationship. (Truth About Deception, 2022) Sexual and emotional infidelity are not the only issues when it comes to divorce and emotional pain. A study published in the *Journal of Sex Research* found that *the probability of divorce roughly doubled for married Americans who* used pornography. (Perry, Schleifer, 2017) An additional study found that pornography use can diminish the effects of connection and intimacy by taking the brain's natural chemical process and "supercharging" it—making the natural release of bonding chemicals in a relationship seem underwhelming. (Voon, et.al, 2014) Whatever the statistic, it is apparent that betrayal from infidelity, in any form, can greatly damage a relationship and can have negative impacts on the mental health of both parties involved.

Terms Used in This Book

Throughout this book, we use several terms that require some definition. These have been included in the Glossary section at the back of the book. We encourage you to take a few moments and go through them in order to prevent confusion as you read along.

PART 1

Intimacy Avoidance and Betrayal

In Laura's classes and groups for partners, she outlines the different types of betrayal we encounter regularly in our practice. These are sexual infidelity (a.k.a. "cheating"), emotional infidelity (a.k.a. "emotional affair), and infidelity through pornography. In the first section of the class, she cites intimacy avoidance as a complicating factor to the issue of infidelity in a relationship. We see intimacy avoidance as a unique type of betrayal because the intimacy avoidant person is so concerned with protecting themselves that they betray their partner by withholding themselves on multiple levels. Terms often used to describe the phenomenon of intimacy avoidance are intimacy anorexia®, a term coined by Dr. Doug Weiss, narcissism or narcissistic relationship (not to be confused with Narcissistic Personality Disorder), sexual anorexia, and sexless marriage. If you are unsure whether or not intimacy avoidance is complicating your situation, here are some common symptoms of this issue:

- Can't seem to commit fully to the relationship

- Often holds the partner to impossible, unattainable standards

- Is perfectionistic and/or feels unlovable when they themselves aren't perfect

- Stays so busy with work and projects that they have little time to spend with their partner

- Has little to no trust for their partner, even if they have earned it

- When issues/arguments arise, the person's first response is to put the blame back on their partner

- Has little to no empathy

- Plays the victim, especially after being confronted with wrongdoing on their part

- Seems distant during sex or regularly avoids sex

- Makes sexual performance a condition of staying in the relationship

- Acts like listening to their partner's feelings is a huge imposition and/or extremely taxing

- Seems overly sensitive to criticism (real or perceived)

- Dismisses their partner's valid issues and emotions with a "just get over it" attitude

- Refrains from showing love to their partner in ways they know the partner needs or appreciates

- Refuses to praise or compliment their partner

- Is unwilling or unable to share true feelings with their partner

- Uses anger, disapproval, and/or silence as a means to control or punish their partner

- Has ongoing or ungrounded criticism of their partner and verbalizes it, or frequently seems silently judgmental

- Gets overly angry and/or defensive when challenged

The reason we feel that it is important to bring up intimacy avoidance right after the introduction section is that, if this is an issue, rebuilding trust in the relationship becomes significantly more complicated. In relationships struggling with intimacy avoidance, intimacy and trust have been absent for most of the relationship's duration. Ongoing gaslighting, devaluation, and minimization are typically present, which means that trust needs to be rebuilt, or built for the first time, on multiple levels because it has been broken down by these things in addition to the other types of betrayal. As outlined in the definitions section, the term "gaslighting" describes a subtle or overt form of manipulation in which the gaslighter attempts to sow seeds of doubt in their partner's mind about the validity of their emotions and reality. This is done in an attempt to shirk responsibility for bad behavior and is always at the expense of the person being gaslighted. Some examples of gaslighting can include saying something wasn't said when it was, presenting an image of being a caring person in public while acting uncaring and unempathetic at home, and telling a person that they are exaggerating when their feelings have been hurt—effectively invalidating that person's experience.

Partners of intimacy avoidants often blame themselves for the problems in their relationship. This is because the gaslighting and minimization they have experienced is a form of emotional and mental abuse that erodes a person's trust in their own perceptions. They tend to take on too much responsibility in response to their partner's lack of accountability. Oftentimes, their thinking has become muddied from years, and sometimes decades, of gaslighting. This can lead the wounded partner to take on responsibility that isn't theirs when it comes to rebuilding trust—and the intimacy avoidant is often happy to let them do it. When a person struggling with intimacy avoidance is caught in infidelity-related behavior, it is not at all uncommon for them to blame their partner in an attempt to avoid taking personal responsibility for their actions. As a result of years of systematic emotional abuse in the form of gaslighting, devaluation, and undermining, it is common for a partner of an intimacy avoidant to accept, at least in part, the responsibility for their partner's behavior.

It is important that we point out that, no matter what the circumstances, our stance is that the partner who engages in infidelity-related behavior is 100% responsible for their choice to be unfaithful. Although all relationships have issues and no one is perfect, the idea that anyone is forced into acting unfaithfully is ludicrous. Infidelity is never a viable option for dealing with problems, either real or perceived. There are many choices that the wounding partner could have made besides engaging in infidelity-related behavior. With the intimacy avoidant, blame shifting, for infidelity or for other bad behavior, is par for the course. This is extremely damaging and can even be dangerous for a wounded partner who believes that all they need to do is to work harder at forgiveness and/or on themselves in order to "save" the relationship. Meanwhile, the intimacy avoidant, who is the source of the issue, escapes accountability.

We have worked successfully with many couples dealing with betrayal when intimacy avoidance is a complicating factor. That being said, we feel it is important to point out that the intimacy avoidant's behavior must be dealt with as urgently as any issues arising from betrayal if trust is ever to be rebuilt. In relationships where intimacy avoidance is present, infidelity is only *one* of the serious problems that a couple faces. These relationships are commonly riddled with issues such as lying, undermining, gaslighting, demeaning, and invalidation that must be dealt with along with the damage done from the betrayal itself. It is imperative that the intimacy avoidant both face and change these bad behaviors along with their infidelity-related behaviors if the relationship is to be considered a healthy one. It is also important to note that ongoing accountability is important before the partner of an intimacy avoidant can determine if trust should be extended. Unfortunately, many intimacy avoidants are especially adept at doing and saying the right things, at least in the beginning, in order to avoid the consequences of their behavior. Only time will tell if they are truly remorseful for what they have done and are willing to do the recovery necessary to change their ways. This includes building empathy, which intimacy avoidants typically lack, in order to see things from the wounded partner's perspective.

PART 2

The Rebuilding Trust Pyramid

There is a lot of information out there when it comes to rebuilding trust in relationships. Our challenge was how to break it down into a simple form so that our clients could understand the overall process. In the end, we created the Rebuilding Trust Pyramid. The four layers of this structure include honesty, safety, consistency, and intimacy. While this book is specific to rebuilding trust after betrayal, we feel that the pyramid can be applied to most romantic relationships, friendships, and even family relationships where a breach of trust has taken place. Let's take a look at each of these layers in detail:

Figure 1: The Rebuilding Trust Pyramid

Honesty

Honesty is the foundation of trust in all healthy relationships. Without honesty, relationships fail to thrive. When we work with wounded partners, they often tell us that the lies they were told by the wounding partner are just as hard, if not harder, to move past than the infidelity-related behavior. Lying, for most wounded partners, represents multiple betrayals. These betrayals often make them feel disrespected and foolish. Not only did the wounding partner break the agreement that was between the couple when they engaged in the infidelity-related behavior, but they lied about it. In many cases, the wounding partner has been lying for quite some time. This causes the wounded partner to call into question everything that happened before and after the lies were told. They now question who their partner is as a person because lies demonstrate selfishness, a major character defect, on the wounding partner's part. The fact that the wounded partner may not have realized the depth of this character defect often causes them to conclude that they don't know the wounding partner at all. Additionally, the wounded partner also questions whether the wounding partner ever really loved them. This creates an excruciatingly painful situation that is difficult for the wounded partner to wrap their head around.

Lying also creates an imbalance in the relationship. The wounded partner assumed that their partner was as committed to the relationship as they were. However, the betrayal and the lying causes them to question whether or not their partner ever truly gave their heart to them at all. Every word, every action, every holiday, every meaningful event, every sexual encounter now all seem suspect. The question in the wounded partner's mind becomes, "If you could do this and lie about it, is everything else also a lie?"

Finally, lies punctuate the intentionality of infidelity. Much of the wounding partner's infidelity-related behavior can be at least partially explained by things like addiction, self-centeredness, immaturity, etc. However, the fact that the behavior was intentionally covered up by the wounding partner's lies is something that can't be explained other than to say that the wounding partner knew, on some level, that what they were doing was wrong. The calculated nature of lying highlights the fact that, to some extent, the actions engaged in by the wounding partner were deliberate. This feels highly personal to the wounded partner. In our work, we are often told by wounded partners that they don't feel like they know their partner anymore, and that maybe they never did. This indicates a profound loss of trust—not only in the wounding partner, but in the soundness of the relationship and even in life as they knew it to be.

If a couple is to have a chance at rebuilding their relationship after betrayal, it must be built on a foundation of honesty and transparency. Ongoing lying and dishonesty will send the wounded partner the message that the wounding partner is primarily concerned with their own comfort, even if it is at the expense of the wounded partner's heart. This is seen as, and is in fact, another betrayal. If honesty cannot be established, what remains is a relationship devoid of trust and intimacy.

Safety

Although honesty can help build safety in a relationship, in the case of betrayal, more needs to be done in order to achieve this. When we speak with wounded partners who have been hurt by their partner's infidelity-related behavior, they almost always describe feeling unsafe. First and foremost, this is because the predictability of the relationship is now gone. This typically initiates a fight or flight response from the wounded partner because the wounding partner's actions have caused betrayal trauma. Unfortunately, it can take the wounded partner weeks and months (in some cases longer) before their body and mind stop reacting to the trauma. Safety in the relationship must be reestablished if the wounded partner is ever to get out of a hyper vigilant mode of operation. In the case of relationships where intimacy avoidance is present, safety may never have been properly established in the first place. This is because partners of intimacy avoidants often feel an overall lack of acceptance from their partner and, therefore, never felt safe to begin with.

When betrayal occurs, it can cause a lack of safety in several areas. The types of safety that are most often violated are physical/sexual, emotional, and commitment. Other types of safety that may be affected can include community standing (when the discovery of infidelity-related behavior causes a loss of status or friends), financial (when the wounding partner spends money on their infidelity-related behavior), and even personal (when the wounding partner shares details of the relationship or the family with an affair partner). An area where safety can be damaged *after* infidelity has been disclosed or discovered is in the area of communication. This typically happens through inappropriate displays of emotions (such as name calling or shaming), stonewalling, defending, and threatening. During group and individual intensives, we work with couples at length to establish plans to address the different areas where safety has been violated and needs to be restored.

Consistency

Considered to be the "meat and potatoes" of recovery from betrayal, consistency is key if trust is truly to be rebuilt. Consistency is an important ingredient to trust because it shows the wounded partner that they can depend on the wounding partner to follow through. When we work with couples to develop plans to create safety, we always explain that, without consistency, those plans are basically useless. When the wounding partner engages in infidelity-related behavior, they send a message to the wounded partner that they can't be trusted to uphold the promises and agreements that are important to the health of the relationship. If the wounding partner wants their partner to accept that they can change this, they must be consistent. Anyone can profess remorse and make promises, actions speak louder than words. If the day-to-day actions of the wounding partner include defensiveness, a lack of accountability, ongoing lying (even about seemingly small things), playing the victim, and criticism, the wounded partner receives the message loud and clear that their partner lacks the commitment necessary to rebuild trust. The result is that the chance of rebuilding trust diminishes. The proof of the wounding partner's commitment to do whatever it takes to restore the relationship lies in their day-to-day behavior. The consistency phase of rebuilding trust is ongoing and takes the longest time to establish.

Intimacy

When we think of intimacy, people tend to jump straight to sex. Although this is one type of intimacy and is often an expression of other types, it is not the only one. Some common areas of intimacy that a couple can share are created by sharing emotions, resolving conflict successfully, sharing goals and dreams, sharing and respecting each other's thoughts and opinions, connecting around religion and spiritual ideas and beliefs, and sharing hobbies and interests.

The feelings of devastation, betrayal, loneliness, ambivalence, and confusion caused by betrayal cause a breakdown in intimacy between partners. One of the reasons for this is because these feelings can cause one or both parties in the relationship to withdraw. Although this is common for a period of time when infidelity is discovered or disclosed, both partners will need to recommit to the relationship if trust is to be restored. In the case of relationships where intimacy avoidance is present, little to no intimacy was present in the relationship prior to the discovery or disclosure of a betrayal. When we test couples for the strength of their relationship structures (more on this later in the book), we typically find that most of these are completely missing. The issues caused by intimacy avoidance, intimacy anorexia®, and generally self-centered behavior leave the relationship weak. Adding betrayal to this already weak structure makes it extremely difficult for couples dealing with these issues to survive unless the intimacy avoidant is willing to admit to the totality of their bad behavior and begin recovery right away.

The fact that intimacy is at the top of the Rebuilding Trust Pyramid is a bit deceptive as it implies that intimacy will not be developed until honesty, safety, and consistency are completely in place. The truth is that intimacy will be built all along the recovery journey, and that the "ingredients" of honesty, safety, and consistency are what produce intimacy. When we think of it this way, the diagram looks like this:

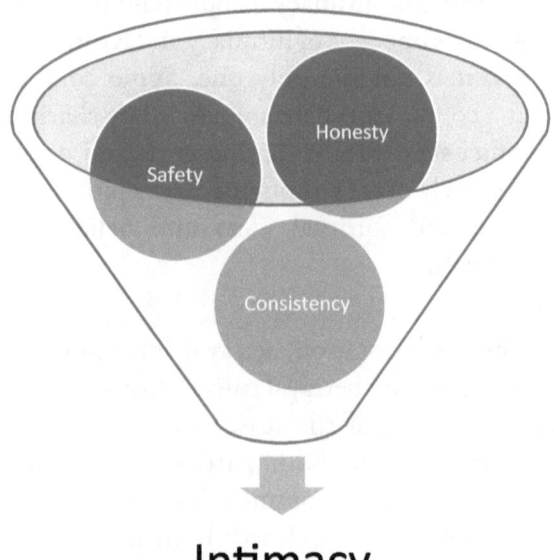

Intimacy

Figure 2: Ingredients of Intimacy

The building of intimacy in a relationship is an ongoing process. Intimacy is like a plant that grows over time as each person in the relationship gives it what it needs in order to thrive. It is not a destination that, once reached, can be checked off the list and ignored. When any of the ingredients to intimacy are missing in a relationship, it fails to thrive and, ultimately, dies on the vine. It must be constantly watered and nurtured if it is to remain. This is the work of commitment within a relationship. For the purposes of this book, however, we will be addressing intimacy as a separate element in order to give you ways in which you can actively nurture it.

PART 3

Rebuilding Trust Pyramid Layer #1

Honesty

"I'm not upset that you lied to me, I'm upset from now on I can't believe you."—Nietzsche

We would like to preface this section on honesty by stating that much of the information contained here will be directed at the wounding partner. Although both parties play an active role in rebuilding trust, it falls to the wounding partner to do much of the work in the beginning stages because they are the one who broke the trust by engaging in infidelity-related behavior. In our experience, if a wounding partner is granted a chance to regain trust from the wounded partner, how they respond to that chance is crucial to trust being rebuilt. If the wounding partner doesn't take this responsibility seriously and put all of their effort toward doing whatever it takes, the relationship can be further damaged. If this goes on for too long, the relationship stands little chance of ever being a healthy one and is more likely than not to end completely.

As we stated in the Introduction section, honesty is the foundation of trust in relationships. Lies and trust can't coexist in a healthy relationship over the long term. When we lie to our partner, we disrespect them by leaving them in the dark and refusing to take responsibility for our actions. We essentially tell them that we consider our own self-interest to be more important than theirs. This leads our partner to feel unloved and uncared for. Lies indicate that we don't put much value on the relationship and, therefore, can't be trusted to take care of it—or of them.

When infidelity is discovered or disclosed, the wounded partner is sent reeling. This is because betrayal injures attachment. It causes intense trauma to a wounded partner because the violation of trust suddenly calls everything—the past, present, and future of the relationship—into question. The bond between the couple, known as a pair bond, is ruptured. (Johnson, 2004) Studies have shown that pair bonds play an essential role in human health because they act as buffers against stress, depression, and anxiety. (Young, 2003) When these bonds are broken, the trauma caused by the break engages the limbic system, which results in a fight or flight response. It is not uncommon for wounded partners to become disoriented and alternate between anxious-preoccupied responses and fearful-avoidant responses. (Cluff-Schade, Sandberg, 2012) Since there are so many systems and hormones involved with bonding, the wounded partner's entire equilibrium is thrown off when infidelity is discovered or disclosed.

Our purpose in telling you this is not to discourage you. Instead, it is to impress upon you the seriousness of the situation. It is our hope that, if you understand what has happened, then the issue of betrayal and the resulting turmoil in your relationship will be given the attention it deserves. Rebuilding trust after betrayal is a long and difficult process that cannot be rushed. Given the information that you just read, we hope you can see why. Trust must be rebuilt brick by brick with intentional effort, and this starts with honesty and transparency moving forward. There are several ways that we work with couples trying to establish honesty as a foundation for rebuilding trust. In order to address the main ones, we have broken them into four categories: trust-building behaviors, trust-breaking behaviors, trust-building beliefs, and trust-breaking beliefs.

TRUST-BUILDING BEHAVIORS

Trust-Building Behavior #1: Complete Disclosure

The first trust-building behavior is complete disclosure. Other than the wounding partner ceasing to engage in infidelity-related behavior, how disclosure is handled is the most crucial part of rebuilding trust. In order to start rebuilding trust, the wounding partner must first trust the wounded partner with the information regarding their infidelity-related behavior. Without complete disclosure, it is very difficult (if not impossible) for couples to make progress in the rebuilding trust process.

Although we highly recommend that disclosure be done in a therapeutic setting with a trained coach or counselor, we do get a number of couples who have attempted disclosure or plan to attempt disclosure on their own. Due to the serious nature of disclosure and the potential damage that it can do to one or both parties in the relationship, **we do not recommend that you attempt disclosure on your own.** The information contained here on the most common mistakes made during disclosure and the guides to what should be included in disclosure and what questions to ask should be used for informational purposes only. **This information is not designed as a do-it-yourself tool.**

Some of you may already be through the disclosure process. For you, we would suggest still reading this section because you may learn something new that could be helpful to you. If you are currently engaged in some of these common mistakes, consider this a chance to correct those. For those of you who have not made it through the process, please read through this section carefully so that you can avoid the most common mistakes made during disclosure.

In order to better prepare you for the therapeutic disclosure process, we would like to highlight the top 3 mistakes that couples make when attempting a disclosure conversation. It may seem counterintuitive, but research shows that the wounding partner's willingness to completely disclose infidelity-related behaviors and answer the wounded partner's questions without defense facilitates healthy recovery. One of the biggest barriers to complete disclosure is the need for the wounding partner to control the flow of information.

Common Mistake #1: Dribble Disclosure

The term "dribble disclosure" is used to describe a situation in which the truth about infidelity-related behavior is "dribbled" out over time. This is usually because the wounding partner fears the wounded partner's reaction to the information. Therefore, the temptation is for the wounding partner to withhold information and release it in smaller chunks. Many times, this is a misguided attempt to make it somehow easier for the wounded partner to handle. Also, if the wounding partner is being honest with themselves, they are often doing it in an attempt to lessen their own consequences. Many wounding partners realize that what they have done is a mistake and have an intense fear that disclosing information will lose them the relationship. The problem with this is that it sends the message to the wounded partner that the wounding partner's primary focus is still on themselves and their own discomfort, instead of on the relationship. Although the wounding partner's fears are understandable, attempts to control the flow of information are misguided.

A research study done by well-known author and infidelity expert Peggy Vaughn found that 72% of betrayed women and 70% of betrayed men actually found the deception harder to get over than the infidelity itself. (Vaughn, 2010) The implications of this study are that, even though details of the infidelity will be hurtful to the wounded partner, the deception around infidelity and disclosure is far more damaging to the rebuilding of trust. This is why dribble disclosure is so harmful to the recovery process. Each time the wounding partner holds back critical information, they are deceiving the wounded partner yet again. When this is done, it lessens the chances that the wounded partner will recover in time to be able to participate in the process of rebuilding trust. Each experience amounts to a new deception and betrayal to them. This essentially cuts their legs out from under them in terms of their journey toward recovery.

The other issue with dribble disclosure is that it communicates the message that the wounding partner is still disloyal. When information is withheld, it is usually because the wounding partner is being more loyal to themselves and/or their infidelity partner(s) than they are to their wounded partner. This is like pouring salt into a cut. The truth can serve to realign loyalty in the relationship. Dribble disclosure undermines this.

Common Mistake #2: Believing that disclosure will make things worse

Although it may seem futile to disclose information and answer questions because it will likely end up in a fight, anger, or tears, nothing could be further from the truth. Withholding information from the wounded partner regarding something that has deeply affected their life is not only controlling, but also unfair and even cruel. Without the necessary information, the wounded partner will likely deal with one or more of the following:

- An inability to trust again because they can't make sense of the information in order to help them recover
- Constant triggers from unresolved trauma

- A feeling that the entire history of the relationship has been tainted because they don't understand the extent of the betrayal

- An inability to trust their own judgement because they don't know how they have been deceived

- Hyper-arousal from constant worry and fear of danger

- A feeling of being robbed of having an authentic relationship

- A feeling of foolishness for staying with the wounding partner

- A feeling of being doubly wounded. First, by the betrayal and second, by the withholding of information

- A feeling of needing to protect themselves, ensuring that the wounded and wounding partners will never be on the same page in the relationship.

Additionally, the wounding partner is likely to experience one or more of the following:

- A sense that their partner would never love them if they really knew what they have done

- Repeated infidelity-related behavior because the first behavior was kept in the dark and never dealt with

- Anxiety over the wounded partner finding out what has happened

Failure to completely disclose infidelity-related behavior will also likely result in one or more of the following consequences to the relationship and/or family:

- A marked increase in recovery time
- Prolonged emotional instability
- Additional trauma
- A feeling of chaos due to a failure to create safety
- The possible destruction of the parts of the relationship that are good
- Decreased possibility of relationship recovery
- Increased fighting
- Increased potential of children being hurt in the process

Common Mistake #3: Giving too many or too few details

It is important to note that the disclosure process **should be driven by what the wounded partner needs to know**. The wounding partner must be willing to submit to this idea if rebuilding trust is going to be possible. Answering the wounded partner's questions plays a vital role in the recovery process. Without answers, the wounded partner is likely to think on the subject night and day. Their mind is likely to run wild with possible scenarios that never happened.

It is not uncommon for wounded partners to ask an extraordinary amount of questions. For most, asking more and more details is their way of trying to get a handle on the situation. With patience and honesty on the wounding partner's part, the intensity of question-asking should lessen over time.

That being said, it is important for the wounded partner to carefully consider what they truly need to know. A detail, once known, cannot be unknown. Two common ways in which the wounded partner can be further wounded while asking questions is if 1) they ask questions that may cause them to compare themselves with others or 2) too many "why" questions that prolong the disclosure process. Although it is important to understand why the betrayal happened, too many "why" questions early on can lead to frustration because the wounding partner is often not self-reflective enough to understand the "why" themselves. We do, however, recommend that the wounded partner ask at least some "why" questions early on to give the wounding partner the opportunity to answer them. Though, the wounded partner should not be surprised if the answers change over time as the wounding partner gets more recovery and is able to reflect on their motives in a deeper manner.

The following is a list of detailed information that we recommend **should not be included in the disclosure process**:

- Graphic or explicit details regarding specific sexual behavior

- Names of affair partner(s), unless they are known to the wounded partner

- Specific locations where the wounding partner engaged in infidelity-related behavior, unless the locations are within the circle of safety (see Glossary definition) of the wounded partner

- Specific fantasies (it is okay to disclose that the wounding partner fantasizes during sex, but it is not recommended to get into specifics)

We want to make it clear that the disclosure process should be driven by what the wounded partner feels they need to know in order to make decisions about how to proceed in the relationship. We can't stress the fact enough that **it isn't up to the wounding partner to decide how much the wounded partner gets to know**. That being said, the list above was put together based on our experience as to the types of information that are typically the most damaging. As stated above, once a detail is known, it cannot be unknown. Explicit, graphic, and/or unnecessary details will only serve to create more triggers for the wounded partner and will almost certainly prolong the recovery process. We have had experience helping multiple couples where the wounded partner's knowledge of explicit details was the nail that sealed the coffin of the relationship because they could not move past it.

As a general rule, it is not a good idea for the wounded partner to ask questions in the heat of the moment. We advocate at least a 24-hour evaluation period prior to asking questions. Our advice is for the wounded partner to write down any questions they may have and commit to not asking them for a minimum of 24 hours. Additionally, we advise that the wounded partner ask themselves the following questions about each question to determine whether or not they truly need to be asked:

1. Why do I want to know the answer to this question?

2. Will the answer to this question help me recover? (yes or no)

3. If yes, how will the answer to this question help me recover?

If the answer to a particular question will not aid in the recovery process in any significant way, we advise that the wounded partner strike it from the list of questions.

For many wounded partners, asking more and more details is their way of trying to get a handle on their situation. They mistakenly believe that if they just find out one more detail, they will finally make sense out of what has happened to them. Sadly, the truth is that there will be a portion of the betrayal that they may never make sense of. For most wounded partners, this inability to make sense of the wounding partner's behavior stems from the fact that they could never fathom doing what their partner has done themselves. Most wounded partners that we work with would never betray their partner in the way that they have been betrayed. The fact that the wounding partner could set them and the relationship aside in order to engage in infidelity-related behavior is unfathomable. Asking more questions will do very little to explain the disparity between how the wounding partner thinks and how the wounded partner thinks. It is a sad fact that the wounding partner's behavior was selfishly motivated, and this will never make sense to someone who's primary loyalty is to their partner and the relationship.

PART 4

Preparing A Disclosure

As we stated above, we recommend that disclosure be made in the presence of a trained coach or counselor and the information detailed here should not be used as a do-it-yourself guide. That being said, we would like to offer you some guidance as to what information should be included in a disclosure as well as what types of questions we recommend for the wounded partner to ask.

In an effort for the wounding partner to get honest with the wounded partner, if they haven't already, the following can be used as a guideline to prepare a document containing the facts of the infidelity-related behavior. Typically, the information contained in a disclosure consists of any infidelity-related or addictive behavior that the wounding partner engaged in after having entered into a committed relationship with the wounded partner. However, in many cases, it is important that details of certain behavior that was engaged in prior to the commencement of the relationship be included as well. This holds especially true if the wounding partner has an addiction to sex or pornography and/or if they misrepresented themselves to their partner at all during the relationship. Some examples of this include when the wounding partner has a history of cheating or pornography use that wasn't disclosed, was lied about, or was minimized. This also holds true if the number of sexual partners the wounding partner had prior to meeting the wounded partner was lied about. Since the wounded partner likely engaged in the relationship based on the information provided to them by the wounding partner, the lies (either blatant or by omission) represent a significant betrayal of trust.

Although the disclosure process should be driven by what the wounded partner needs to know in order to heal, here is a rough outline as well as some examples of information typically included. For your reference, we have included a disclosure guide that outlines behavior engaged in prior to the wounding partner's relationship with the wounded partner as well as one that does not include that information. It is important to note that, when working on disclosure with a trained counselor or coach, they will likely have their own format for you to use.

Sample #1
Nature of the Betrayal

- Type of betrayal
- Frequency of contact
- Types of contact
- Approximate money spent
- Lies or gaslighting involved

Timeline

- From _____ to _____, I engaged in _____ approximately _____ per week/month

- From _____ to _____, I engaged in _____ approximately _____ per week/month

- From _____ to _____, I engaged in _____ approximately _____ per week/month

Examples:

From January – April of 2021, I engaged in a texting relationship with a co-worker. We texted approximately four times per day during this time. We discussed our relationships with our spouses.

From April of 2021 to December of 2021, I engaged in a sexual relationship with a coworker. We met twice per week at their house and had sex.

From December of 2017 to January of 2020, I engaged in a sexual relationship with an escort that I found online. We met once per month at a hotel. The approximate money I spent on this was _____.

Clarifications

Please also make a list of what your harmful behavior did/did not involve:

- Involve unprotected sexual intercourse

- Impact our family's safety (e.g., texting while driving, giving out personal identifying information, having people in our home)

- Occur in our home

- Involve individuals that you know

- Risk a loss of job or legal consequences

- Exposure of the infidelity to our children

Devices, apps, and websites used

To pave the way for future accountability, the wounding partner should make a list of the following:

- Website name
- App name
- Laptop
- Cell phone
- Work computer

Sample #2
Masturbation

Started age:

Ended age or last time:

Places (types of place not names of places):

Frequency: ___ per week

Most common associated co addictions:

Pornography/Sexually Stimulating Images

Started age:

Ended age or last time:

Places (types of places not names of places):

Frequency: ___ per week

Most common associated co addictions:

Forms used (videos, etc.):

Sites used:

Strip Clubs
Started age:

Ended age or last time:

Places (types of places not names of places):

Frequency:

Money spent:

Drugs
Started age:

Ended age or last time:

Types of drugs

Frequency:

Money spent:

Phone Sex
Started age:

Ended age or last time:

Types of Places/Locations (not names):

Frequency:

Money spent:

Online Chat Rooms
Started age:

Ended age or last time:

Types of Places/Locations (not names):

Frequency:

Money spent:

After Relationship Affairs

Started age:

Ended age or last time:

Number of different people

Of those, how many were 1 time with same person

Of those, how many were 2-6 times with same person

Of those, how many were over 6 times with same person

Types of Places/Locations (not names):

Anyone your partner knew

Ever in home, their/your vehicle etc.

Protected or unprotected sex

Are you currently in contact with any

Last time you were in contact with any

How you met them

Money spent:

After Relationship/Commitment Paid Sex

Started age:

Ended age or last time:

Number of different people

Of those, how many were 1 time with same person

Of those, how many were 2-6 times with same person

Of those, how many were over 6 times with same person

Types of Places/Locations (not names):

Anyone your wife knew

Ever in home, her/your vehicle etc.

Protected or unprotected sex

Are you currently in contact with any

Last time you were in contact with any

How met them

Money spent:

After Relationship/Commitment Emotional Attachments/Affairs

Started age:

Ended age or last time:

Number of different people

Of those, how many were 1 time with same person

Of those, how many were 2-6 times with same person

Of those, how many were over 6 times with same person

Types of Places/Locations (not names):

Anyone your partner knew

Ever in home, their/your vehicle etc.

Protected or unprotected sex

Are you currently in contact with any

Last time you were in contact with any

How met them

Money spent:

Pre-Relationship Sexual Relationships Misrepresented/ Not Disclosed

Started age:

Ended age or last time:

Number of different people

Things not involved (Answer yes or no)

None of our Children involved or know

Friends or family members

No STD symptoms

Was never in love or fantasy of love

No underage contact or fantasy

No homosexual contact or fantasy

No animal contact or fantasy

Secret devices, bank accounts

In order to pave the way for accountability moving forward, the wounding partner should disclose any devices they have kept hidden from the wounded partner as well as any hidden bank accounts.

If the wounding partner used other means to engage in infidelity-related behavior, they should include it. Just because the option doesn't appear in this document doesn't mean it should be left off. Remember, a lie by omission is still a lie. We would like to stress that the wounding partner should never leave something off the disclosure with the assumption that it isn't going to be a big deal. We guarantee that it will be a big deal. An example of this is when a wounding partner leaves pornography use off of their disclosure assuming it won't be a big deal in comparison to 3 sexual affairs that were previously disclosed. **All relevant information to addiction and infidelity-related behavior must be disclosed.** When it comes to relevancy, the wounded partner should be the one to decide what is relevant and what is not.

Admitting to Manipulation, Lying, and Gaslighting

To assure that the disclosure process is truly complete, the wounding partner will need to take full ownership for the unfair and painful ways they have tried to manipulate the situation so that their infidelity-related behavior would not be discovered or called into question. For many wounded partners, the lies told by the wounding partner are even more painful than the betrayal itself because it made them doubt their ability to read the situation correctly. This often leads to an erosion of confidence as well as a diminished capacity for trusting themselves.

These include:

- Outright lying

- Becoming defensive and angry when questioned

- Playing the victim and acting like the wounded partner had done the wrong thing by asking questions or being suspicious

- Acting hurt by the questions that were being asked

- Omitting crucial information and details about whereabouts and activities

- Acting like the wounded partner was crazy or was imagining things that were actually true

- Initiating fights or arguments to avoid having to talk about it

- Deleting browser histories, using separate devices, and the like to cover the wounding partner's tracks

- Blaming the relationship or the wounded partner for the wounding partner's distance from them and/or the family

- Blaming the wounded partner for the wounding partner's infidelity-related behavior

- Fault finding as a way to detract from the issues

In order to help the wounded partner heal, the wounding partner not only needs to own up to the above-listed behaviors, but will also need to commit to eliminating lying, blaming, shaming, rage, and manipulation from the relationship in the future. This is especially true of relationships complicated by the factor of intimacy avoidance. Trust cannot be rebuilt if these behaviors are not eliminated because they cause a lack of safety in the relationship.

PART 5

Trust-Building Behavior #2

Polygraph

The second trust-building behavior is the wounding partner's willingness to take a polygraph examination. In our experience, the polygraph is a powerful instrument that can help pave the way to rebuilding trust in a relationship because it can provide a couple with a baseline of truth when there has been deception involved. Polygraphs are helpful to the wounded partner because they address the issue of ongoing lying on the part of the wounding partner. Unfortunately, due to the deception involved with betrayal of any kind, the wounded partner is often at a loss as to what to believe moving forward. Since the wounding partner has proven that their words cannot be trusted, the polygraph provides a powerful, objective tool by which the wounded partner can measure the wounding partner's statements and, hopefully, move forward toward reconciliation. Polygraph examinations can also be a useful therapeutic tool for the wounding partner because, when used on an ongoing basis, the examination can help deter relapse. We have talked with countless wounding partners that have told us that the polygraph helped keep them honest in the beginning stages of recovery in a way that neither we nor the wounding partner could. Infidelity-related behavior, especially when combined with addiction, is not an easy thing to overcome. Ongoing polygraph examinations can help with this because, sometimes, the fear of getting caught is the only thing that keeps certain people honest in the beginning. The polygraph can be the tool these people need to gain recovery until they develop the discipline and emotional capacity to deal with life in a way other than engaging in infidelity-related behavior. For ongoing accountability, our recommendation is that the wounding partner take a minimum of two polygraph examinations in the first year, two the second year, and one per year thereafter or until the couple decides polygraphs are no longer needed. Please be aware that we recommend that polygraphs be done at least once per year indefinitely when sex addiction and/or pornography addiction are present.

It is important to note that we always consider the use of polygraph examinations to be at the discretion of the client. That being said, we highly recommend them for couples struggling to rebuild trust because lying is such a difficult thing to detect. Although we consider ourselves competent in the areas of infidelity, addiction, and intimacy avoidance, we can never be 100% sure whether someone is lying or not. We have had discussions with many of our colleagues around this, and they feel the same way. Even though polygraphs have their limitations, they are still valuable as a therapeutic tool to address honesty in the disclosure process and ongoing accountability for the wounding partner. Additionally, sometimes even the mention of a polygraph can serve as a tool to help wounding partners get honest and/or help the wounded partner gauge the willingness for their partner to do whatever it takes to help rebuild trust. A common question that we get asked by the wounding partner is, "If I don't remember everything, will it show that I am lying?" It is important to remember that a polygraph doesn't test memory. It only tests whether or not the wounding partner is being deceptive about not remembering. If the wounding partner truly doesn't remember certain things because their memory is fuzzy from the passage of time, addiction, or substance use, the polygraph will not typically show deception.

We want to stress that the polygraph should never be used by the wounded partner as a means of punishment for the wounding partner's actions. Polygraph examinations are most useful in rebuilding trust when both partners agree to use them for the good of the relationship. It is important to note that polygraphs, especially the initial one, can be extremely anxiety provoking for the wounding partner. Therefore, it is important that they engage in the polygraph process willingly for the benefit of the relationship. It is also important to note that polygraphs are not a replacement for empathy and compassion on the wounding partner's part. Although polygraph examinations are a useful tool in helping a couple rebuild trust after betrayal, they are not the most important. Empathy, compassion, a lack of defensiveness, expressions of remorse, and a willingness to be self-reflective are all critical if the relationship is to be restored. If the wounding partner goes into the polygraph process kicking and screaming and continues to be angry that they had to take one, the polygraph loses a lot of its benefit. This is because, even if they pass the test, the wounding partner's attitude is direct evidence that they are still primarily concerned with their feelings and comfort, instead of with their partner's. Conversely, if the wounded partner refuses to accept the results of the polygraph as valid, the test loses its value as well. We have seen this a handful of times with clients that choose to believe their own version of the truth instead of being open to the fact that what they believe may be based more in emotion than in fact.

The polygraph examination itself consists of three parts: the pre-test, the polygraph examination, and the interpretation of the results. The cost varies between polygraph examiners but usually ranges between $300 to $700. Currently, most polygraph examiners use computerized polygraph instruments, although there are a few out there that may still use the old fashioned analog devices. The computerized polygraph systems can score tests better and more consistently than humans and are, therefore, considered to be superior to analog instruments. When conducted properly, the American Polygraph Association (APA) states that polygraph tests are approximately 90% accurate, although critics claim this percentage is more like 75%. (Iacono, Ben-Shakar, 2019) There is also a new credibility assessment tool called EyeDetect that has been used in the market since 2013. It uses an infrared camera to measure pupil dilation, blink rate, and other eye movements. This system is automated, fast, and gives results (after a 30-minute test) in about 5 minutes. (Converus website) The makers of EyeDetect claim that it can provide up to 90% accuracy, although the APA states that the accuracy is approximately 83%. For therapeutic purposes, we prefer to use live polygraph examiners because we feel that the human touch gives better overall results in the case of fidelity testing.

Most people experience at least some stress and discomfort when lying. The amygdala, which is part of the limbic system and responsible for processing strong emotions, picks up on the fear associated with lying and with getting caught. Once it senses stress, the amygdala sends a distress signal to the hypothalamus. The hypothalamus then activates the sympathetic nervous system by sending signals through the autonomic nerves to other parts of the body. (Harvard Health, 2020) The autonomic nervous system controls involuntary actions such as heart rate, blood pressure, and pupil dilation. The polygraph was designed to detect some of these physiological changes that happen when a person is lying.

The pre-test is the longest portion of the polygraph examination. Although all polygraph examiners use their own method when conducting the pre-test, most will get at least some background information on the wounding partner. Typically, the polygraph examiner asks the wounding partner if and how they prepared for the test (to check for knowledge of countermeasures) and gets a history of addiction and/or infidelity-related behavior. They also go over terminology used in the questions in order to make sure the wounding partner is comfortable with how they are phrased and/or understands the questions' meanings. It is also not uncommon for the polygraph examiner to have a conversation with the wounded partner in order to understand what they are most concerned with knowing or what they are particularly nervous about.

After the pre-test, the examiner places sensors on the wounding partner's fingers, arm, chest, and abdomen in order to measure physiological changes in blood pressure, pulse, and rate of perspiration. Some polygraph examiners will also use sensor pads that they place on the floor. These are used to measure movement in the feet and legs, which can also be associated with lying. Once the equipment has been set up and the sensors put in place, the polygraph examiner will then ask the wounding partner a series of control questions. The testing period will also include questions that the subject will be asked to answer with a false statement in order to gauge how their body reacts when they are lying. Once the control questions have been asked, the polygraph examiner will then ask the questions relevant to the test. The number of questions asked should be no more than four. Asking more than four questions typically decreases the accuracy of a polygraph, according to the APA.

It is highly recommended that you work with a trained professional who understands the therapeutic polygraph process when you are trying to decide which questions should be asked. When we work with couples, we help them draft four relevant questions that adhere to the following guidelines:

- **Time Bound**: When polygraph questions are time bound, they leave far less room for error. An example of a time-bound question is, "Since August 2, 2012, have you engaged in a sex act outside of your marriage?"

- **Yes or No**: Polygraph questions should be designed in such a way that they can be answered with yes or no. Asking questions that require any other type of answer will turn up an inconclusive result.

- **Behaviorally Focused**: Questions around motives and/or emotions are not appropriate for a polygraph. For example, the answer to a question like, "Do you love me?" will likely turn up an inconclusive result. A question like the example above is more appropriate for a polygraph because it focuses on a specific behavior—in this case a "sex act".

We understand that the wounded partner will likely have a lot more than four questions that they need answers to. However, the polygraph examination is not the time to get those answers. When we work with couples, we encourage the wounded partner to prepare questions that they want answered ahead of time. The wounding partner then answers these questions during the disclosure process, and the polygraph is then used to verify whether or not the wounding partner told the truth during the disclosure.

Once the polygraph examination has been completed, the examiner will typically inform the subject as to whether they passed or failed. If one or more of the wounding partner's answers show deception, the polygraph examiner will inform the subject of the issue(s) and dig deeper into why a particular answer might have been deceptive. If the wounding partner gives the polygraph examiner new information to help explain discrepancies, the polygraph examiner will then conduct a confirmation test in order to determine whether or not the new information supplied by the wounding partner explains, in full, the deception. If working directly with our office, the polygraph examiner will then discuss the results with us as well as with the wounded partner. For this to happen, the wounding partner will need to sign a release of information prior to the commencement of the polygraph examination. The polygraph examiner will require the wounding partner to sign other types of paperwork as well.

At Becoming Well, we work closely with the American Polygraph Association to vet any and all polygraph examiners that we send our clients to. In addition, we perform an interview with potential partners in order to determine if they are a good fit for the therapeutic polygraph process. Part of what we are looking for is an examiner who understands the difference between therapeutic polygraphs and criminal ones. Criminal polygraphs are designed to catch those who have committed criminal acts and often involve a stressful atmosphere in which the subject doesn't know which questions they are going to be asked. In the therapeutic polygraph process, wounding partners are fully aware of what questions they are going to be asked ahead of time. If the couple is working directly with us, these questions will have been decided on in a process that includes the couple and ourselves. We find that polygraph examiners that have a gruff exterior and/or act like everyone is guilty until proven innocent add unnecessary stress to the process, and we tend to weed them out. We also ask questions to determine if the potential examiner understands the polygraph guidelines and laws in their state as well as if they run a 2-chart minimum. We currently work with verified polygraph examiners in major cities all over the U.S.

When we work with couples who are considering polygraph examinations as a way to start to rebuild trust, the most common objection we hear is that couples don't want to base their relationship on the results of a polygraph. Our answer to this is that no one should ever base their relationship on the results of a polygraph. Other behaviors such as a willingness to be accountable, empathy, and compassion are even more important than taking a polygraph. Without these, the wounding partner passing a polygraph test will do very little to aid in the rebuilding of trust. As we stated earlier in this section, polygraph examinations are always used at the discretion of the client. The choice of whether or not to use one in your recovery journey is a highly personal one that can only be made by you. That being said, we feel that an unwillingness to take one on the wounding partner's part, especially if the wounded partner has requested it, is quite telling. Although it doesn't necessarily indicate that they are still lying (although in many cases it does), it shows a lack of willingness to do whatever it takes to mend the relationship.

PART 6

Trust-Building Behavior #3

Expressing Remorse

The third trust-building behavior is the wounding partner's ability to express remorse for what they have done. The words "I'm sorry" are a good start but do very little to help the wounded partner if they are not accompanied by action. In their book *The 5 Apology Languages: The Secret to Healthy Relationships*, authors Gary Chapman and Jennifer Thomas define the 5 apology languages as:

- Expressing regret (saying I'm sorry)
- Accepting responsibility
- Making restitution
- Genuinely repenting (changing behavior)
- Requesting forgiveness

When we work with couples, we work with the wounding partner to help them understand the apology language of the wounded partner. This is because apologies mean very little when the person apologizing is not speaking the language of the person being apologized to. Although every person has their preference as to the way they like to receive an apology, in the case of betrayal, we find that the wounding partner's apology needs to encompass all 5 of the apology languages plus statements that indicate self-reflection as well as the expression of empathy for the wounded partner.

So what do we mean by remorse? We define remorse as a strong feeling of regret, grief, or sadness when contemplating one's past actions that compels one to admit to their guilt and to change behavior moving forward. The fact that true remorse involves action separates it from the feelings of guilt and shame. It is particularly important to point out that the self-pity that often accompanies guilt and shame are usually not received well by the wounded partner and do nothing to heal the relationship. This is because self-pity keeps the focus on the wounding partner instead of on the wounded partner and comes off as self-serving and defensive. Remorse, as opposed to guilt and shame, requires action in order to communicate it. Here is a formula that the wounding partner can use for expressing remorse:

1. Start off with an apology, stating the specific action(s) that you are apologizing for (expressing regret)

2. Express understanding for at least some of the attitudes that led to these actions (expressing self-reflection, accepting responsibility)

3. Express understanding for how your actions have affected your partner (expressing empathy, taking responsibility)

4. Ask your partner for forgiveness (requesting forgiveness)

5. Explain that you understand why it is important that you change your behavior moving forward (expressing self-reflection, taking responsibility)

6. Ask your partner what you can do to show them that you are truly sorry (making restitution)

7. Do what your partner asks you (expressing genuine repentance, taking responsibility)

8. Commit to making changes (accepting responsibility)

9. Follow through with your commitment to change (expressing genuine repentance)

A true expression of remorse requires that the wounding partner take 100% responsibility for their infidelity-related behavior without asking the wounded partner to accept any of the responsibility for it. As demonstrated in the formula above, it also requires that the wounding partner express at least some understanding of the mindset, attitudes, and entitlement that led to the infidelity-related behavior. As the wounding partner's recovery deepens, deeper awareness will develop over time. It is important to note that the presence of addiction will often hamper the wounding partner's ability to conduct the self-evaluation necessary to express true remorse, which can make the overall process slower. This is because, in order to engage in actions associated with addiction, the wounding partner had to justify those actions in their own mind first. This led to several layers of denial that will need to be addressed if true recovery is to take place. A lack of remorse often indicates the emotional immaturity that typically accompanies addiction. When an addict uses substances, sex, pornography, etc. to deal with their emotions, this stunts emotional growth. This lack of emotional maturity can make it difficult for them to see things from another person's point of view. A lack of remorse is also common in situations where the infidelity-related behavior was not disclosed by the wounding partner but was, instead, discovered by the wounded partner. This is because the wounding partner may not have been ready or willing to own up to their bad behavior prior to getting caught. If either of these scenarios describes your situation, it is important that you work with a trained coach or counselor that can help the wounding partner work on developing empathy in order to gain a new perspective.

If the wounded partner does not see improvement in the expression of remorse as time passes, this should be considered a red flag. When we work with couples, we advise that the wounded partner give the wounding partner a window of time in order to observe their behavior for signs of remorse if they do not see it up front. Of course, the length of the window is a personal decision that a wounded partner must make for themselves. However, our recommendation is about six months. Here are some of the positive changes a wounded partner should see in a wounding partner that is remorseful for their actions:

- A willingness to earn trust slowly

- Increased awareness of motives and attitudes that drove the infidelity-related behavior

- A willingness to accommodate requests from the wounded partner regarding accountability and actions

- A willingness to embrace the consequences of their actions

- An attitude of humility

- An attitude of patience toward the wounded partner when they are expressing their feelings and/or asking questions

- The development of discipline/self-control

Conversely, here are some of the attitudes of a wounding partner that wounded partners should consider to be red flags:

- Displays of anger and resentment when actions are called into question

- Defensiveness in the form of stonewalling, blame, or excuses

- Displays of entitlement, such as complaining about the consequences of their actions or demanding forgiveness

- Displays of self-pity, such as moping or the silent treatment

- Deflecting the need to be accountable by acting like they are the victim or wallowing in self-pity

- Making excuses for their behavior, blaming the wounded partner, or blaming other people

As stated previously, many of these behaviors may be present when the wounding partner is caught in their infidelity-related behavior and/or addiction is present. However, if the wounding partner is serious about saving the relationship, these should dissipate within the six-month window of recommended time. If a wounding partner is truly interested in reconciliation, they will need to accept the consequences of their actions without blaming the wounded partner or demanding that they "just get over it" and trust them. Trust has to be earned. Demanding trust comes from a place of dishonesty and deception. It indicates that the wounding partner is still in denial of how much their actions have hurt their partner and has, therefore, deceived themselves. This self-deception is indicative of an attitude of entitlement and, often, of active addiction and/or narcissistic attitudes. Entitlement, defensiveness, and a lack of remorse do not support reconciliation.

Trust-Building Behavior #4: Answering Repeated Questions with Empathy

The fourth trust-building behavior is a willingness on the wounding partner's part to answer the wounded partner's repeated questions with patience, empathy, and compassion. When the wounded partner finds out about the wounding partner's infidelity-related behavior, life shatters into a million pieces. Everything they have built their life on up to this point feels like a lie and they are left scrambling to put the pieces back together in a way that makes sense to them. The problem is that making sense of the wounding partner's behavior takes time and some aspects of what happened never end up making sense at all. Repeated questioning is the process by which a wounded partner begins to piece their life back together. For the most part, the urge to find out more and more information is driven by the wounded partner's desire to heal. The problem is that, as much as repeated questioning is a normal and necessary part of the rebuilding trust process, it can lead to anger and exasperation on the wounding partner's part for several reasons:

- It reminds them of what they have done. Many times the wounding partner feels a great deal of shame and regret for their infidelity-related behavior. Questioning by the wounded partner provides a constant, unpleasant reminder of how they have failed. A wounding partner who responds in anger to their partner's questions is usually struggling with shame.

- They want to escape accountability. This one, like the first one, is often driven by shame. It can also be driven by feelings of entitlement. In order to escape feelings of shame that might be brought on by accountability, the wounding partner chooses to deflect these feelings by acting angry or exasperated. If entitled, the wounding partner may resent facing the consequences of their actions.

- They don't want to self-reflect. Some wounding partners get very comfortable in their denial because it keeps them from acknowledging how they have hurt someone they love and, as a result, feeling bad. An angry response can be used as a smokescreen in order to avoid self-reflection.

- They have resentments. It is not uncommon for wounding partners to build up resentments against the wounded partner for real or perceived wrongdoing. If this is the case, the wounding partner will need to engage in coaching or counseling with a trained professional in order to work through their feelings.

- They are still engaged in infidelity-related behavior. Angry responses don't always signify guilt but, when accompanied by other behaviors, they can indicate ongoing behavior that the wounding partner feels guilty about.

- Their answers make no difference. Unfortunately, sometimes wounded partners ask questions and then don't accept the answers. This is understandable when the wounding partner is stonewalling or trying to avoid accountability. However, when the wounding partner is honestly trying to answer questions to the best of their ability, an unwillingness to listen on the wounded partner's part can be extremely frustrating and discouraging.

PART 7

Asking Questions

While on the subject of answering repeated questions with empathy, we want to take a moment to address the wounded partner's need to ask questions. When there has been betrayal of any type in a relationship, the questions that need answers are many. Regardless of type, questions center around who the behavior was with (in the case of emotional and sexual affairs), how and when the infidelity-related behavior began, details surrounding the behavior, if the behavior has ended or is ongoing, what the wounding partner is willing to do to make sure it doesn't happen again, and the "why" questions. Let's take a closer look at the 6 categories of questions we just described:

1. Who Was it With?

It is only natural for the wounded partner to want to want to know who their partner has been unfaithful with in the case of either sexual or emotional infidelity. However, we urge the wounded partner to use caution here. Asking questions pertaining to "who" are only useful when it comes to what has happened within the wounded partner's circle of safety. Asking these questions about someone they don't know can cause more harm than good. The reason for this is that asking questions about someone not known to the wounded partner often causes natural curiosity to kick in. We have seen partners get stuck for months looking up pictures of people they don't know. This often leads to unfair comparisons and using their energy to beat themselves up about perceived shortcomings compared to the other person(s). Additionally, partners often waste precious emotional energy seeking after information about total strangers that would be better spent on themselves and/or on their relationship. Finding out what an affair partner looks like, what their hobbies are, etc., while tempting, is unproductive. We recommend that the wounded partner ask themselves what they can possibly know about this person that would make any difference to the situation with their partner.

A better question for the wounded partner to ask the wounding partner up front would be, "Do I know this person?" If the answer is yes, then we recommend following up with a question around who the person is. Knowing who the person is makes a lot more sense if it has been established that the wounded partner knows them first. It is important for the wounded partner to understand if they know those involved because people within the circle of safety present a more complex issue for them. This is because more than one betrayal has taken place: betrayal from their partner as well as betrayal from someone close to them. Additionally, a lack of knowledge as to who this person is can cause a situation in which the wounded partner inadvertently has ongoing contact with someone who has had an inappropriate relationship with their partner. This can be an extremely unsafe and violating experience.

2. How and When Did It Begin?

In order to begin to comprehend what has happened, it is important that the wounded partner understand the circumstances surrounding their partner's infidelity-related behavior. The answers can vary depending on the nature of the infidelity. Typically, infidelity through pornography or betrayal through intimacy avoidance is something that wounding partners carried into the relationship themselves. In our experience, most of these behaviors started long before the wounded partner ever entered the picture.

Here are some examples of appropriate questions to ask:

- When did the infidelity-related behavior start?

- How did the behavior start?

- Who initiated it? (if an affair)

- How long have you been viewing pornography and/or sexually stimulating images?

- How did you start viewing pornography and/or sexually stimulating images?

- How long have you been masturbating to pornography and/or sexually stimulating images?

- How long have you been aware that you've been withholding love from me?

- Were you aware that you had an issue with this prior to our relationship beginning?

- How long have you been gaslighting me? Were you aware that you were doing it?

These are only some examples of the many questions that could be asked in this category. We recommend that the wounded partner write any questions pertaining to "how and when" down and then wait at least 24 hours before asking them.

3. Details of the Infidelity-Related Behavior

This category can be tricky. The wounded partner will want to keep in mind that, while it is important to understand the basic outline of the infidelity-related behavior, too many details will create unnecessary triggers that they don't need.

Examples of good questions to ask are:

- How often did you meet this person?

- How often did you have sex?

- Was protection used?

- How often are you viewing pornography/sexually stimulating images and masturbating?

- Why do you feel that it's acceptable to withhold from me?

- Did it ever occur to you that I was suffering from your withholding?

- Did you ever reveal details about me or our family?

- Where are you accessing pornography and/or sexually stimulating images?

- Where did you find people to have an affair with?

- How much money have you spent on these activities?

- How much time do you spend on this weekly?

- Are you keeping any mementos?

- How did you contact this person/these people?

The list of questions in this category is endless. It is important for the wounded partner to realize that they will never likely understand everything about the wounding partner's activities. The goal is for them to understand enough of the basic idea of what went on to make informed decisions regarding the future.

We would also like to give you an idea of the types of questions that are what we refer to as "Danger Zone" questions. These questions, when asked and answered, can re-traumatize an already-wounded partner as well as lead to an increase in intrusive thoughts and triggers.

- Questions pertaining to specific sex acts, positions, etc.

- Questions pertaining to certain locations that might create a trigger for the wounded partner later on (i.e. specific hotels, cities, etc.)

- Questions regarding details such as hair color, body part sizes, etc.

- Questions pertaining to "dirty talk"

- Questions about lingerie, sex toys, etc.

- Questions pertaining to whether they preferred the affair partner's sexual performance to yours

- Questions like, "What do they have that I don't have?"

It is important for the wounded partner to remember that this is not about them. This is about the wounding partner and their poor choices. The wounded partner did nothing to deserve this. Asking questions that might lead them to feel bad about themselves or blame themselves somehow won't help. The wounding partner could have chosen other ways to behave and, instead, chose to act unfaithfully. It is important that the wounded partner put the blame where it belongs.

4. Is the Behavior Ongoing?

In the work we do, we have found that whether the wounding partner is willing to end the infidelity-related behavior is the number one determining factor as to whether a couple will reconcile or not. Relationships fail when the wounding partner isn't able or willing to change their ways

In our experience, most wounded partners want to know if there is any infidelity-related behavior that is ongoing. Here are some helpful questions to ask:

- Has the affair ended? If so, when did it end? Who ended it?
- Are you still in contact with the infidelity partner? If so, how do you communicate?
- Do you love this person?
- Do you still look at pornography and/or sexually stimulating images? When was the last time you looked at pornography/sexually stimulating images?
- Do you intend to end the infidelity-related behavior?
- If you haven't ended the behavior, why not?

These are just a few of the questions that the wounded partner might have regarding the wounding partner's intentions and activity.

5. Future Intentions

When considering reconciliation with an wounding partner, it is important for the wounded partner to understand what safeguards their partner has put in place to help ensure that the behavior won't happen again. If the wounded partner discovered their partner's infidelity-related behavior, then the wounding partner won't likely have had time to think about what they should do to get and stay in recovery. In this case, the wounded partner can ask questions about what the wounding partner is willing to do instead. Here are some good questions to ask:

- Have you been STD tested? If not, are you willing to do so?

- Do you still want to be with the other person?

- Have you blocked your access to pornography/sexually stimulating images?

- Do you still want to withhold yourself from me?

- What are your reasons for telling me?

- Do you hope we can reconcile?

- Are you being completely honest?

- Is there anything I haven't asked that you should tell me? (This is a particularly great question because it highlights the fact that information, when withheld, is dishonesty and should be considered another form of betrayal)

- What steps have you taken to block your access to this person, to the porn, etc.?

- Are you willing to join a recovery group?

- Are you willing to do an intensive?

- Are you willing to take a polygraph test?

- Do you feel guilty?

6. The" WHY" Questions

The answers to this category of questions are often the most disappointing and frustrating for wounded partners. This is why we recommend that you limit the number of questions you ask in this category. Understanding why seems so key to putting their life back together, yet many of the answers to "why" elude them.

One of the primary reasons for this is that the wounding partner rarely knows why themselves, at least in the beginning stages of recovery. This is especially true in the case of sex/pornography addiction as well as intimacy avoidance.

Early on, wounding partners typically have very little insight into their own behavior. One of the main reasons for this is because, in order to commit betrayal, they had to justify their behavior in their own minds first. This typically leads to several layers of denial that will have to be worked through during recovery. Additionally, someone who has been unfaithful may not feel great about themselves. Poor self-image can lead a person to become defensive when questioned because they're afraid of what the answers might say about them.

Denial and justifications are especially prevalent where addiction is concerned. In order to support the addiction, the wounding partner had to compromise themselves and others around them. Many addicts feel intense shame about their behavior and acknowledging that behavior, especially in the beginning, can be extremely difficult for them. IAs and pornography/sex addicts, in particular, tend to have a marked lack of empathy as well. This is especially hard for a wounded partner who needs to know that their partner understands how they have been hurt and cares about it.

Lack of empathy is a sign of emotional immaturity, and addicts and intimacy avoidants are typically less mature than they should be. Emotional maturity develops, in large part, when we must find healthy ways to deal with intense and/or unpleasant emotions. People emotionally mature when they have to struggle to find a resolution within themselves or when they seek trained professionals to help them grow. When someone has an addiction to sex or pornography or even to withholding themselves from their partner, they go to the addiction time and time again to soothe themselves. In many instances this addictive behavior becomes their primary coping mechanism for all of life's ups and downs. They don't have to deal with life on life's terms and overcome problems because the addiction masks the feelings and gives them an alternative. This leaves them emotionally immature and unable to handle things such as conflict, criticism, and changes they have no control over. It also leaves them with a lack of self-reflection because of the layers of denial it takes to stay in addiction. The very nature of addiction is to "numb out" or escape emotions. As addiction progresses, it muddies the addict's thinking and makes it difficult to evaluate or control their own behavior. Asking someone with little to no self-awareness to explain to you why they did something will often lead to frustration.

If this describes your current situation, as a wounded partner, we want to tell you that we completely understand the pain that you are in. We also want to give you hope that, as the wounding partner moves through recovery, they will likely emotionally mature and gain empathy in the process. The work done in recovery is all about self-reflection, which can develop relatively quickly once addiction and numbing-out behavior is removed. Our best advice to you as the wounded partner is that you join a support group and/or see a trained professional that can help you work through some of the "why" questions that the wounding partner isn't currently able to answer.

We most often see wounded partners get stuck in the questioning stage of discovery around the "why" questions. Although it can be helpful to understand why someone did something, it can be highly frustrating when they say that they don't know why or when their answers don't seem to make much sense. Many times, wounded partners simply must come to the realization that they may never fully understand their partner's reasons for doing what they did. In order to move forward, the wounded partner might have to accept the fact that they may never be fully satisfied as to why something happened the way it did and that their partner's confounding behavior will remain, to a point, somewhat of a mystery.

PART 8

Final Thoughts on Trust-Building Behaviors

Something that we would like to mention before closing this section on trust-building behaviors is that there is a big difference between the wounding partners who truly don't understand their own behavior and, therefore, give mediocre answers as to "why" and those who are using the answer "I don't know" as a way to get the conversation over with quicker. If you are reading this book as a wounding partner and you are doing the latter, we want to impress upon you that stonewalling your partner in this way will lead to a further lack of trust in the relationship and will, more likely than not, ultimately contribute to the relationship's demise.

As we explained previously, repeated questioning by the wounded partner is a normal part of the rebuilding trust process. We find that these questions often fall into one of five categories:

- Shock: Questions like, "how could you do this?" and "do you have any idea of how much you have hurt me?" are indications that a wounded partner is struggling to comprehend the situation. When infidelity-related behavior is discovered or disclosed, the losses associated with that knowledge initiate the grieving cycle. A wounded partner asking these types of questions is struggling with the first stage, shock.

- Putting the facts together. This is the most common

category of questioning. As we explained previously, when betrayal is discovered or disclosed, it shatters the wounded partner's world. Asking questions about who, what, where, when, and why and getting the answers are a crucial part of the recovery process.

- Testing motives and mindset. Questions that fall into this category sound like, "do you love them more than me?" and "do you wish you could still be with them?" Although these are a normal part of the questioning process, we don't recommend these types of questions because they can lead to additional triggers and unfair comparisons.

- Rapid fire. There are times when the wounded partner asks a series of questions and doesn't seem to wait for the answers and/or doesn't seem to care about the answers given. In our experience working with wounded partners, this category of questions is more about expressing hurt and anger than it is about getting answers. Instead of engaging in this type of questioning, we recommend that wounded partner get in touch with what they are feeling and work that through with their partner or with a trained coach or counselor.

- Reflective. These are the most vulnerable types of questions and usually don't come until late in the recovery process. Although the wounding partner is 100% responsible for engaging in infidelity-related behavior, the wounded partner is likely aware that they aren't perfect. They may start asking questions in order to ascertain what might have gone wrong in the relationship. Although this can lead to deep and productive conversations between partners, it isn't likely to happen until the wounding partner accepts full responsibility for their actions without blaming the wounded partner.

It can be helpful for the wounding partner to understand the motives behind the different types of questions so that they can answer in a way that helps the wounded partner heal.

How the wounding partner responds to their partner's questions is key to the rebuilding trust process. If the wounding partner engages in any of the following behaviors, they will likely further damage their partner and the relationship:

- Stonewalling by giving the silent treatment or refusing to answer.

- Raging and acting indignant.

- Minimizing the wounded partner's emotional pain.

- Playing the victim and acting hurt or going into shame by saying they are a terrible person.

- Blame-shifting by claiming that the wounded partner wasn't meeting their needs or by pointing out the wounded partner's imperfections.

- Justifying by using addiction as an excuse or saying that stress caused the infidelity-related behavior.

- Prolonged ambivalence. This is expressed when the wounding partner doesn't know what they want. If the relationship is to stand a chance of recovery, both partners must fully commit to working on the rebuilding of trust.

The ability for the wounding partner to respond to the wounded partner's questions with empathy, patience, and compassion is key to the rebuilding trust process. Aside from full disclosure and honesty moving forward, this element is probably the most important determining factor as to whether or not trust will ultimately be rebuilt. One of the main reasons for this is that, when the wounding partner does not show empathy, compassion, and patience to the wounded partner, fighting tends to escalate and those fights tend to remain unresolved. Prolonged, unresolved conflict will tear at the fabric of an already-fragile relationship and eventually destroy whatever hope there is left of saving it.

When the wounded partner asks repeated questions, they are likely trying to resolve the immense pain that they are in. It can be hard for some wounding partners to grasp the extent of their partner's emotional pain, and this can, unfortunately, lead them to minimize it. Studies suggest that when we experience rejection, our brains react similarly to when we experience physical pain. Scientists hypothesize that this is because a human being's best chance for survival is within a group. Therefore, rejection is a very bad thing. (Whitcomb, 2021) A 2003 study done through UCLA monitored participants' brains by fMRI while they played video games with peers. When participants were excluded from the game, the scans showed that the brain experienced distress and, as a result, blood flow to the anterior cingulate and insular cortices was increased. (University of California, 2003). This is the same blood flow pattern that occurs when people feel physical pain. As human beings, we feel intense pain when we are rejected—and there is possibly no worse rejection than being set aside while our partner gives their heart and/or body to someone else or chooses to withhold love from us. If you are a wounding partner who is wondering whether or not your partner's pain is real, let us assure you that it is.

So, how can a wounding partner show empathy to the wounded partner? If you are a wounding partner reading this, here are some ways that a person can convey empathy and concern:

1. Own and lead the recovery process. It is important that you own your recovery and that you take responsibility for it. Reading articles and sharing them with your partner, making a coaching or counseling appointment on your own, and sharing insights about what you are learning are all things that will help the wounded partner know that you are taking your recovery work seriously.

2. Take ownership of your infidelity-related behavior. This doesn't mean that you have to take responsibility for every

problem in the relationship but taking responsibility for your infidelity-related behavior without defending yourself or blaming your partner is key to showing that you understand and care about your partner's feelings.

3. Ask the wounded partner to write you a letter. If you are having a hard time being empathetic, ask your partner to write you a 2-3-page letter explaining their feelings. After reading it and processing the information, come back to them and validate their emotions.

4. Deliberately engage in conversations. A common mistake made by wounding partners is that they often avoid conversations that the wounded partner wants to have about the pain they are experiencing. This can happen through refusing to answer questions, saying "I don't know" without attempting to answer to the best of their ability, or physically leaving and/or staying away. Instead, hang in there with your partner and listen to what they have to say. Better yet, commit to starting some of the conversations by asking how they are doing.

PART 9

Now that we've wrapped up trust-building behaviors, we would like to discuss the most common trust-breaking behaviors we see in our office.

Trust-Breaking Behavior #1

Failure to End Infidelity-Related Behavior

Whether it be a sexual affair, emotional affair, looking at pornography, or intimacy avoidance, the wounding partner's lack of willingness to end the infidelity-related behavior is the number one reason why couples are unable to reconcile after betrayal has been discovered or disclosed. We would like to preface this section by stating that we understand that ending infidelity-related behavior is not always an easy thing to do. That being said, it is the wounding partner's responsibility to show a commitment to recovery by getting help to end whatever they have gotten caught up in. In our experience, it is not possible to effectively work on a relationship in the long-term if the wounding partner continues to engage in infidelity-related behavior.

The "grass is always greener" mentality is a common issue when it comes to infidelity, especially in the case of sexual and emotional affairs. It is not uncommon for us to hear from a wounding partner that they feel justified with continuing their behavior because their partner is the source of their problems, and that their affair partner meets their needs in a way that their current partner cannot. The idea that engaging in infidelity-related behavior will do anything to resolve issues for the wounding partner, whether real or perceived, is a fallacy. Infidelity does not cure problems. Instead, it creates them. We hear from wounding partners on a regular basis about how they thought that engaging in infidelity-related behavior would help ease their relational and/or personal problems but, instead, are now left with new problems on top of the old ones. Although infidelity in the form of affairs, pornography, and withholding can offer temporary fixes for unpleasant experiences and emotions, they are not a solution to them. The problems of life must be dealt with head-on if they are truly to be resolved. If the wounding partner continues to act out with infidelity-related behavior, they are only temporarily drawing attention away from their issues. The wounded partner is not the source of their problems. In committed relationships, our partner only highlights the problems that are already within ourselves. Therefore, we must each take responsibility for addressing our own issues and reach out for expert help when we need it. Otherwise, we fall into the victim mentality which says that we don't have to be responsible for fixing our issues because other people are responsible for causing them and, therefore, for fixing them.

Infidelity provides a fantasy land for the wounding partner. It offers a temporary fix for the emotional impact of life's problems. In the case of emotional and sexual affairs, a powerful concoction of neurochemicals are stimulated when limerence or infatuation are present. These are often mistaken for true feelings, or even love. The neurotransmitters involved in infatuation and limerence are part of the brain's reward system. The release of these chemicals causes an intense reaction in the brain that feels like true love but is only the biological reaction that we get during the infatuation stage of love. As most of us know, the infatuation stage is only temporary. However, in the case of affairs, this stage can be prolonged because of the adrenaline involved in the excitement and stress of sneaking around. Let's take a closer look at the main chemicals involved with infatuation and limerence:

- Epinephrine: Also known as adrenaline. Epinephrine makes your heart beat faster, blood pressure rise, and your breathing quicken. Epinephrine is associated with effects on the heart.

- Norepinephrine: Associated with the fight or flight response. Norepinephrine is similar to epinephrine and is also closely related to dopamine. Norepinephrine is associated with effects on the blood vessels.

- Dopamine: Associated with the reward system of the brain. Known as the "feel good" hormone, dopamine is associated with pleasure and libido. It also motivates focus and action.

- Serotonin: Levels of serotonin drop during infatuation, leading to obsessive-type thinking about the other person when we first feel infatuated with someone.

- PEA: Phenylethylamine, or PEA, is known as the "love molecule". It is associated with the flood of chemicals that enter our brain during infatuation and acts as a natural amphetamine that causes us to focus intently on our feelings. (Savulescu, Sandberg, 2008)

The presence of this powerful cocktail of chemicals helps explain why the emotions experienced during affairs can feel so real. This can make them difficult to end. Another reason why affairs are often difficult to end is that the wounding partner tends to perceive the affair partner as kinder, more affectionate, more supportive, and more attentive than the wounded partner. The problem is that these perceptions come about because of the wounding partner's fantasy, which is based on an artificial situation. The pressures of a mortgage, children, illnesses, in-laws, and the tough things that come with life's struggles over time are all absent in the fantasy land of an affair. Research shows that affairs typically don't last and, if they do somehow end up in marriage, the divorce rate is approximately 75%. (Pittman, 1990)

A word about limerence

We would like to preface this section by explaining our use of the term "limerent object" to describe an affair partner and/or someone who the wounding partner is infatuated with. This term is not meant to devalue this person in any way. Instead, the word "object" is applied to the subject of the wounding partner's limerence to explain how they are being viewed by the wounding partner. In limerence, the limerent object is being objectified by the other person. As opposed to being viewed in their totality and being loved warts and all, the limerent object has become a subject of a person's fantasy. As a result, they are being idealized in an unrealistic way which is based on the need of the wounding partner to escape reality.

According to the Glossary found in this book, we define limerence as "a strong state of emotional infatuation, longing, and even obsession that lasts as little as 6 months and as long as 3 years." In her book *Love and Limerence: The Experience of Being in Love*, author Dorothy Tennov observed the following features about limerence:

- Frequent intrusive thoughts about the limerent object who is a potential sexual partner

- Increased time spent with or ruminating on the limerent object

- An intense need for feelings to be reciprocated

- Exaggerated mood dependent upon the limerent object's actions (despair when rejected, elated when feelings are reciprocated)

- Temporary relief from unrequited feelings through fantasy about the limerent object

- A desire for exclusivity with the limerent object

- The ability to downplay the limerent object's faults while emphasizing their positive features

- Feelings for the limerent object are intensified through adversity

What makes limerence especially powerful is the fact that the wounding partner's attraction is often based on things or traits that they perceive they lack for themselves. The subject of the limerence is idealized as having the exact attributes that the wounding partner feels that they are lacking in themselves and/or in their relationship. Limerence is very self-focused in the way that it is about getting something rather than giving something. Wounding partners who are experiencing limerence will need attention, sex, and validation from the limerent object because it fulfills their fantasy. The behaviors of a person in a state of limerence are similar to those of an addict. In the case of limerence, the wounding partner becomes intoxicated with another person in a similar way that alcoholics become intoxicated by using alcohol. In order to punctuate the similarity, here is a list of characteristics commonly associated with those engaging in substance abuse:

- An inability to give up a substance

- Keeping a steady supply of the substance

- Withdrawing from important relationships

- Spending a large amount of time pursuing the substance

- Constantly thinking about the substance

- Engaging in risky behavior

- Not being deterred by negative consequences of substance use

- Engaging in secrecy and deception in order to hide the substance use

- Neglecting responsibilities of work, home, etc.

- Experiencing withdrawal symptoms when the substance is absent

Do these things sound familiar? They should if the wounding partner is engaged in an affair that involves limerence. Since limerence is basically "person addiction", it is a very serious issue that is not easily dealt with. The feelings associated with it feel like real love when, in fact, they are something entirely different. If you or your partner are engaged in an affair where limerence is present, we urge you to seek professional coaching or counseling in order to help break the cycle. That being said, here are some strategies you can use in order to break the grip of limerence:

1. Cut off all contact. Any engagement with the object of your limerence will only serve to exacerbate the problem. Avoid any situation or person that is associated with the limerent object. Avoid texting, calling, engaging social media, and any other form of contact with this person.

2. Engage with someone who is objective that can help you see the situation for what it is. If you are in a state of limerence, you will not see things clearly. It is important that you engage the help of a trained coach or counselor, trusted friend, spiritual leader, or mentor who you trust have your best interest at heart and to give you sound advice.

3. Replace the behaviors. As with addiction, it is important that you replace the behaviors associated with limerence with new, healthy behaviors. This can be something like exercise but can also be something like making a list of the wounded partner's strengths and positive attributes.

4. Concentrate on the flaws. This isn't meant to be mean. However, much of the problem associated with limerence is that you are likely idealizing this person while simultaneously

minimizing their flaws. Make a list of flaws (even if it's just one) and pick one to concentrate on instead of indulging your fantasies about this person.

5. Be accountable. Since the hold of limerence is exceptionally strong, you will need to enlist outside help in order to stay accountable. We recommend that you engage someone other than your partner who will call you on it when you are not taking recovery seriously and/or are making excuses or indulging addictive behavior.

Similar to emotional and sexual affairs, pornography use also creates a type of fantasy land for the user. In this fantasy, the person using porn gets all their sexual needs met without having to give anything in return. The object of their pornographic lust and fantasy is always interested, ready, and able to fulfill all their sexual desires and curiosities. Their sole purpose is to please them sexually and, when that particular fantasy no longer meets their needs, another fantasy is just a mouse click away.

The use of pornography for sexual purposes usually involves masturbation and a resulting orgasm. This is problematic not only in the relationship, but for the person using pornography as well. During sex, orgasm, and even afterwards, three extremely powerful, mood-boosting chemicals are released – dopamine, endorphins, and oxytocin. Dopamine plays a major role in reward-motivated behavior. Pornographic scenes are hyper-stimulating triggers, which ultimately lead to unnaturally high levels of dopamine that can't typically be reproduced in a long-term, committed relationship. As a result, satisfaction during a normal, healthy sexual encounter can be viewed as failing to meet expectations. Additionally, this constant release of powerful chemicals during viewing and, ultimately, orgasm leads to the wounding partner bonding with the process of porn usage instead of with the partner.

We often see intimacy avoidance (IA) in combination with pornography. The escapism offered by pornography is particularly attractive to the IA wounding partner because the need to escape is amplified in someone dealing with this issue. This can be confusing to the wounded partner, especially if the IA is sexually anorexic within the relationship. However, if you remember that the primary motivation of the IA is to keep distance from their partner in order to avoid potential pain, it makes sense. Pornography and masturbation allow the IA to have their sexual needs met without any risk of connection to another human being. We see other forms of infidelity in combination with IA as well, but they are not as common as porn usage. For the IA, everything is about driving enough distance between themselves and the partner that they no longer feel in "danger" of getting hurt. If intimacy avoidance is an issue in your relationship, it is important that this aspect is dealt with properly because the presence of intimacy avoidance typically drives infidelity-related behavior. Additionally, even if the IA stops the porn usage, affair, etc., they are likely to treat the wounded partner exactly the same as when they were engaging in the infidelity-related behavior if this root issue is not dealt with.

PART 10

The role of boundaries

In a situation where the wounding partner is unwilling to end an affair or give up other infidelity-related behavior, boundaries on the wounded partner's part are of utmost importance. When the wounded partner fails to set boundaries appropriate for the situation, they are unwittingly empowering the wounding partner to keep engaging in the infidelity. Unfortunately, when wounding partners act this way, they are showing a profound lack of empathy that keeps them from seeing the wounded partner's pain. While they may observe the pain that their partner is in, they continue to minimize it to justify their actions. The wounded partner's lack of boundaries continues the wounding partner's self-delusion that everything is all about them. This unhealthy situation is highly unlikely to change until the wounding partner starts to experience the pain of loss because of their actions.

Sometimes, wounded partners mistakenly engage in pursuing a remorseless wounding partner, believing that if they can only get them to understand that they will stop their destructive behavior. Guilting, shaming, threatening, and controlling the wounding partner in order to get them to stop engaging in their infidelity-related behavior will not produce the desired effect. Neither will insisting that the wounding partner recommit to the relationship 100% immediately. Although it makes sense that the wounded partner would engage in these behaviors in an attempt to ease their suffering and save the relationship, they usually have an effect opposite of what was intended. Engagement in these behaviors are likely to drive an unrepentant wounding partner further away from the relationship, especially if limerence is an issue. Demanding and threatening on the wounded partner's part only serves to fuel the remorseless wounding partner's forbidden behavior because it increases the excitement.

As much as the behaviors listed above do nothing to resolve the issue, neither does giving the wounding partner everything they want. When the wounded partner gives the wounding partner more sex, more patience, accepts responsibility that isn't theirs, or engages in sexual behavior that feels uncomfortable to them, they wind up hurting themselves and allowing the unrepentant wounding partner to have their cake and eat it too. Instead, it is better for the wounded partner to draw boundaries with the wounding partner that show them that, if they continue to engage an affair partner, pornography, etc., they can't have both the infidelity-related behavior and the benefits associated with the relationship.

For the wounding partner who refuses to disengage from their infidelity-related behavior, they are unlikely to change until the pain of the consequences associated with their actions supersedes the benefits derived from it. The wounded partner's boundaries can play a pivotal role in helping an unrepentant wounding partner see the error of their ways. That being said, we feel it is important to stress that boundaries should never be used to manipulate the wounding partner's behavior. However, the absence of boundaries will surely enable it. Instead of using a boundary to try and get the wounding partner to stop their behavior, the wounded partner should consider personal boundaries as a way to keep themselves safe. A personal boundary is an imaginary line that separates people from one another in terms of personal space, feelings, needs, and responsibilities. Appropriate boundaries are a critical component to maintaining healthy connections and are especially important to use when dealing with a remorseless wounding partner.

As we stated previously, a boundary is not a way for the wounded partner to try to coerce the wounding partner into behaving the way that they want them to, nor is it a way to punish them. When we work with wounded partners, it is not uncommon for them to misuse boundaries, especially if they aren't used to setting them. Here are some examples of where boundaries often go awry:

- Using boundaries to get your way
- Using boundaries in an attempt to guarantee safety
- Using boundaries as threats
- Drawing boundaries for someone else
- Becoming rigid around boundaries
- Creating boundaries around almost everything

While it is important that the wounded partner not misuse boundaries, it is just as important that they start to put boundaries in where needed. Here are some common areas associated with boundaries in romantic relationships:

Physical Boundaries

Physical boundaries encompass our need for personal space, physical touch, and physical needs such as rest, nourishment, etc. To put it plainly, physical boundaries are about how we want our bodies to be treated. Sharing your physical boundaries with your partner can be helpful to your relationship. Boundaries such as when you need to rest and when you need to be alone are also important to share. Physical boundaries can be violated when someone touches you in unwanted or harmful ways (such as hugging you when you don't want a hug or hitting you) and when a person invades your personal space. An example of a common physical boundary for the wounded partner when betrayal has taken place is when they don't want the wounding partner to touch them.

Emotional Boundaries

Emotional boundaries are all about respecting feelings and emotional energy. They also let us know where we end, and another person begins. For example, if your partner is feeling agitated and you take this feeling on, you may need to put an emotional boundary in place. You can also limit conversations that take emotional energy by setting a boundary around where and when you talk about certain subjects. Emotional boundaries can be violated when someone criticizes, belittles, or invalidates your feelings.

Sexual Boundaries

Sexual boundaries are vital to any healthy romantic relationship. The idea of sexual boundaries in a relationship encompasses a mutual understanding and respect of limitations and desires between partners as well as overall consent. Sexual boundaries can be violated when we are touched in unwanted ways, coerced or pressured into sexual acts that we are uncomfortable with, guilted into having sex, or physically forced. Additionally, the act of sexual infidelity violates healthy sexual boundaries in two ways. First, it violates the agreement of sexual exclusivity between partners. Second, it violates the wounded partner's body when the wounding partner has sex with them after having sex with someone outside of the relationship. Sexual boundaries can also be violated in open relationships when the rules that the couple agrees upon regarding engaging outside parties are not followed.

Intellectual Boundaries

Intellectual boundaries are boundaries that we set around our thoughts, beliefs, and ideas. Respecting the thoughts of others, even if they are different than our own, and asking that ours are respected is important. An awareness of appropriate discussion around beliefs, thoughts, and ideas is also encompassed by the idea of intellectual boundaries. Much like emotional boundaries, intellectual boundaries are violated when a person refuses to respect our beliefs, thoughts, and ideas as well as when we don't respect another person's. This can come in the form of belittling, dismissing, or ridiculing.

Material Boundaries

The idea of material boundaries encompasses money and possessions. Healthy boundaries in this area involve setting limitations around how much of what you possess is shared with others as well as with whom it is shared. Material boundaries are violated when someone takes something that belongs to you without permission or uses something you own in ways and with people that you never agreed to. The most common ways material boundaries are violated when it comes to betrayal are when the wounding partner spends money on their infidelity-related behavior, gives gifts to an affair partner, or invites the affair partner into the family home, car, vacation properties, etc.

Time Boundaries

This type of boundary refers to how someone spends their time. We often violate our own time boundaries when we don't set aside the proper amount of time for different areas of our life or don't prioritize our time. Some ways others can violate our time boundaries are by demanding too much of our time or controlling our time by dictating how we must spend it. Another way our time boundaries can be violated is by someone who continually makes us late for things or keeps us waiting.

Non-negotiables and Ultimatums

Non-negotiables, or "dealbreakers", are important when setting boundaries when the wounding partner refuses to stop engaging in infidelity-related behavior. Where betrayal is concerned, common non-negotiables include:

- Ending the affair and cutting off all contact with the affair partner (often involves giving proof)

- Willingness to take full responsibility for their actions (now and ongoing)

- Willingness to take a polygraph (now and ongoing)

- Willingness to enter counseling or coaching (now and ongoing)

- Willingness to join an accountability group (now and ongoing)

- Willingness to open full access to phone, computer, emails, etc. (now and ongoing)

It is important for wounded partners to understand that it will take a significant amount of time (months and even years) before a relationship can be completely restored after betrayal. Many changes need to take place in both partners, and this takes time and patience. The wounding partner will need to take a hard look at themselves and put much effort into figuring out their reasons for the infidelity-related behavior without blaming their partner. The wounded partner will eventually have to forgive if the relationship is to be truly reconciled—provided that the wounding partner enters recovery. This is why we have included the words "now and ongoing" on so many of the items above. Recovery is a process.

Ultimatums are also an important part of the recovery process. You may have heard that ultimatums are unhealthy and can hurt a relationship. Although this is true in many cases, we believe that ultimatums are appropriate when it comes to ongoing infidelity-related behavior. For example, if the wounded partner has set up healthy boundaries and non-negotiables and the wounding partner keeps crossing them, it may be time for an ultimatum. Ultimatums should be considered last-resort responses to serious boundary violations. Here are some examples of appropriate ultimatums:

- "If you continue the affair, I am going to end the relationship."

- "If you continue to contact the affair partner, I will move out of the bedroom."

- "If you continue to verbally abuse me, I'm moving out."

- "If you discontinue your counseling, coaching, or accountability group I can't trust you, so I need a separation until you resume those things."

The key with non-negotiables and ultimatums is to use them sparingly. Otherwise, the wounded partner runs the risk of their words falling on deaf ears. It is also important to note that the wounded partner should not say they are going to do something in response to a boundary violation if they are not prepared to follow through with it.

Stating boundaries

When it comes to stating a boundary, we like the DESC method of communication created by Sharon and Gordon Bower as outlined in their book *Asserting Yourself*. The letters DESC break down as follows:

Describe the situation.

Express your feelings and observations about the behavior.

Specify what the ideal outcome would be.

Consequences or compromise. If the behavior persists, explain what the consequences will be. Depending on the situation, a compromise could be appropriate as well.

Here's an example of how to use the DESC method:

"I notice that when I say something you don't like you give me the silent treatment. This is hurtful to me, and I don't think it helps our relationship. Ideally, I would like to be able to have an open discussion with you about things that bother me without being given the silent treatment afterwards. If you continue doing this, I'm going to leave the house and do something fun because I don't want to experience that."

Another easy formula for stating boundaries is:

When you (insert behavior)

I feel (insert feeling)

If you (continued behavior)

I will (consequence)

Here's an example of a statement using this formula:

> *"When you continue communication with your affair partner I feel hurt and betrayed. If you continue to communicate with her, I will go to my mom's for a while until you can show me that you've ceased all communication."*

These methods are similar to each other and can both be used to effectively communicate boundaries.

The role of consequences

You may have noticed that the methods referenced above contain consequences. Consequences play an important role when setting boundaries and should be thought of ahead of time. The proper time to use a consequence is after a boundary has been clearly stated and a person refuses to acknowledge it or honor it.

When first communicating a new boundary, we prefer to communicate it without using the consequence portion of the formula. We find that the person being communicated with usually receives what is being said better without the threat of a consequence. However, we still find it helpful to use the formulas in order to decide what the consequence will be beforehand if the boundary is repeatedly violated. Using the DESC method above, this is what the statement would look like when leaving off the "C" portion:

> *"I notice that when I say something you don't like you give me the silent treatment. This is hurtful to me, and I don't think it helps our relationship. Ideally, I would like to be able to have an open discussion with you about things that bother me without being given the silent treatment afterwards. Can we please agree that you will stop doing this?"*

This type of statement with a request at the end gives the person a chance to respond without threat. If they honor your request, that is wonderful. If not, you can always add in the consequence portion when restating the boundary.

Enforceable consequences

When using consequences, make sure that they are something that you have the power to enforce. This means that the consequence: a) doesn't require the other person to do something, b) is something that you are ready and able to follow through on, and c) isn't overly harsh for the situation. If a consequence for a boundary violation requires the other person to do something, it is not enforceable because you can't control what someone else will and will not do. If you aren't prepared to enforce a consequence, pick a different one. By not following through, you are teaching the person that you don't really mean what you say. If your consequences are overly harsh, you may be able to enforce them, but you risk damaging your relationship by building barriers to intimacy.

Common boundary mistakes

Here are a few common mistakes that we see wounded partners make when trying to implement and enforce boundaries:

- Failing to ask for exactly what they want out of fear

- Setting boundaries that they don't believe in or aren't ready to enforce

- Setting boundaries based on what someone else thinks they should do

- Compromising their boundaries as a response to violations (changing boundaries solely based on the fact that the other person refuses to acknowledge or respect them)

- Creating too many boundaries

- Withdrawing love from the person they set a boundary with

- Failing to model the boundary themselves

The goal of boundaries is to give clear communication as to what you will and will not accept. By avoiding these mistakes, you can help ensure that you get your point across in the way you intended.

PART 11

Trust-Breaking Behavior #2

Refusing to Acknowledge Lies, Gaslighting, and Minimizing

The second trust-breaking behavior is a refusal on the wounding partner's part to acknowledge past or ongoing lies, gaslighting, and minimizing. It is not uncommon for us to hear statements from wounding partners such as, "I'm being honest now, why can't my partner just get over it?" or, "It meant nothing to me, I don't understand why it's such a big deal!" When we hear statements like these, it is clear to us that the person making them has no clue as to how their actions have affected their partner. And, if it is clear to us, it will definitely be clear to the wounded partner. These types of statements scream to the wounded partner that the wounding partner is still protecting themselves and is, therefore, untrustworthy.

Gaslighting

When a wounded partner is gaslighted, it causes them to feel confused, powerless, and sometimes downright crazy. This is because gaslighting involves the wounding partner deliberately trying to get the wounded partner to question their reality. For wounded partners, being in a long-term relationship with someone who gaslights creates a prison of psychological trauma, anxiety, isolation, and depression. A refusal by the wounding partner to acknowledge past gaslighting is the same as refusing to give their partner a key by which their prison door can be opened. Eventually, the wounded partner will need to find their own way out of the prison, and that often means leaving the relationship. If you as a wounding partner think that gaslighting your partner is a way to get them to stay with you, think again. Additionally, a refusal to acknowledge past gaslighting is, in and of itself, continued gaslighting. In essence, your refusal to acknowledge the problem denies your partner's reality that something occurred. This is a common tactic known as withholding (more on withholding below). Here are some common gaslighting tactics:

- Countering: Countering involves the questioning of someone's memory of events

- Withholding: Pretending not to understand what someone is talking about or refusing to accept the validity of someone's experience

- Forgetting: Pretending to have forgotten something or denying that something happened

- Trivializing: Making someone's concerns or feelings seem unimportant or irrational

- Diverting/Blocking: Changing the subject or focusing on the credibility of what is being said instead of the content (Medical News Today, 2020)

Common statements associated with gaslighting include:

- "You never remember things correctly."

- "I never said that."

- "You're being too sensitive."

- "That never happened."

- "I never understand what you're talking about."

- "Your memory is bad. You need to see someone."
- "You seem off. You need help."
- "You're crazy."
- "The kids think you're crazy."
- "This is why you don't have any friends."
- "You can never take a joke."
- "You're the one gaslighting me."

It is important to note that gaslighting is intentional. Therefore, if you are trying to determine whether or not someone is gaslighting you, you need to understand the person's motives surrounding what they are saying. Gaslighting is an *intentional* **behavior directed at diminishing someone's sense of reality or denying their experiences as a way of helping the gaslighter save face**, avoid responsibility, protect ego, or win an argument. "The crux of gaslighting involves a sense of *malice*, i.e., an intentional attempt to deny someone's reality for the gaslighter's gain (even if this gain is subtle or unacknowledged)." (Guha, 2021)

Minimizing

"Arguments of convenience lack integrity and inevitably trip you up."—Donald Rumsfeld

In the quote above, Donald Rumsfeld uses the term "arguments of convenience" to describe the type of arguments that arise from a person's need to argue something that they don't even completely believe themselves because it suits their needs in the moment. Arguments that include minimization on the part of the wounding partner are often arguments of convenience. Although we will concede that wounding partners tend to be unempathetic early in recovery, it is not uncommon for them to eventually acknowledge that they minimize their partner's feelings in an attempt to escape feeling the full consequences of their actions.

The trouble with minimizing is that it essentially tells the wounded partner that their experience, and what they feel as a result, is not a big deal. The definition of the word "minimize" is "to represent at the lowest possible amount, value, importance, influence, etc.—especially in a disparaging way." (Dictionary.com) When the wounding partner minimizes the wounded partner's experience, they are reducing that experience to the lowest possible importance level. Typically, the wounding partner engages in minimization in order to escape feelings of guilt and shame. While this is understandable, it is ill-advised. Some wounding partners who minimize do so because they believe that the consequences of their actions won't be as bad if they can reduce the value of their impact. They think if they can get their partner to concede to the idea that what they did was no big deal, they can get them to move on. This is a way of trying to escape one of the largest consequences of their actions—a troubled and tumultuous relationship. When the wounding partner minimizes the impacts of their behavior, they are taking on a defensive stance. Minimization is only one step away from complete denial of any personal responsibility for the situation. Whatever the reason for using minimization as a tactic, it sends a bad message to the wounded partner for the following reasons:

- It says you are unwilling/unable to accept the consequences of your actions. This sets off an alarm bell with the wounded partner because, if you can't accept consequences, you aren't likely to learn from the situation.

- It shows that you just don't get it. Minimization shows a lack of empathy. It tells the wounded partner that you simply don't understand how your actions have impacted them.

- It says you are willing to throw them under the bus. When you minimize your partner's experience, you are essentially trading the validation of their feelings (something that would help them in their pain) for your own comfort.

- It says that, on some level, you are rationalizing your behavior. In order to minimize the impact of your infidelity-related behavior, you have to rationalize some of it away as not being important.

- It says that you lack the ability to self-reflect. Since minimization is a defensive tactic, it can keep you from doing the self-reflection necessary to truly change your ways.

Minimization is detrimental to the rebuilding trust process because it tells the wounded partner that the wounding partner is still selfishly motivated. When the wounding partner uses minimization as a defensive strategy, the wounded partner receives the message that they are much more interested in saving themselves than they are in saving the relationship. Additionally, minimization tells the wounded partner that the wounding partner lacks integrity. When a wounding partner minimizes, they essentially tell the wounded partner that their lack of follow through on their commitment to the relationship was no big deal. Commitments *are* a big deal. They are an indicator of important character traits such as self-discipline, self-sacrifice, and persistence. A person who is committed is focused and, as a result, is willing to go outside of their comfort zone in order to honor their commitments. A person who lacks commitment lacks focus and, as a result, can end up making hazy choices. When the wounding partner engages in minimization, they show that they haven't changed and that the same character defects that led them to make the decision to engage in infidelity-related behavior are still present.

Lying

Most wounded partners tell us that, as hard as it is to forgive betrayal, it's even harder to forgive the deception surrounding the betrayal. The fact that the wounding partner had a secret life that they knew nothing about can be a hard thing to get over. It is even harder to get over when someone keeps lying. After a while, the wounded partner begins to wonder if the wounding partner is even capable of telling the truth. This can seriously affect their willingness to move forward with the relationship. Additionally, when the wounding partner repeatedly lies, they send the message that they are more interested in protecting themselves than they are in caring for their partner's broken heart.

Trust is pivotal to all healthy relationships. The whole reason we wrote this book was to help couples rebuild the trust that has been torn down by betrayal. Lying and deception not only break trust, but they also lead to more lies and deception to cover up the initial lying and deception. This results in a never-ending, downward spiral that ultimately leads to the complete breakdown of the relationship. Lying also prevents the deep, important conversations that are at the core of committed relationships from happening because distrust can often lead to withdrawal on the wounded partner's part. A lack of communication will also lead to a breakdown of the relationship. Outright lying, half-truths, lies by omission, and even carelessness with seemingly minor details will hamper momentum toward the recovery of the relationship.

PART 12

Trust-Building Belief #1

"I am 100% responsible for my choices."

Now that we have gone through the most common and detrimental trust-breaking behaviors that we see in our practice, let's talk about trust-building beliefs that we consider to be integral to the rebuilding trust process.

The first trust-building belief is the wounding partner's belief that they are 100% responsible for their choice to engage in infidelity-related behavior. Until the wounding partner can accept responsibility for the choices that contributed to their betrayal, progress in the rebuilding trust process will stall out. Many of the behaviors that hamper the rebuilding of trust in a relationship stem from the wounding partner's need to blame, at least in part, others for their choices. This creates a victim mentality (more on that shortly) that hampers connection to self and others. Here are some reasons why accepting responsibility is important:

- It increases confidence. Although many people who refuse to take responsibility for their actions act grandiose, they usually feel the opposite way inside. Working through our mistakes allows us to become free from the guilt, shame, and regret associated with bad choices.

- It allows us to fix your mistakes. It may feel momentarily better to refuse taking responsibility, but we actually disempower ourselves when we do it. Accepting responsibility is the only way to give ourselves back the power to change things.

- It keeps us from damaging others. When we blame other people for our actions, especially a wounded partner, we hurt them emotionally. Taking responsibility keeps us from unnecessarily hurting others that we say we care about.

- It allows us more control over our life. When we take responsibility for our life choices, we can become the author of our own life instead of a victim to everything that happens to us.

When we encounter a lack of willingness to accept responsibility in the clients we work with, it is typically driven from a place of shame. Most of us will profess the fact that we believe the statement that "no one is perfect". However, so many of us don't live it out. Perfectionism and blame can stem from a deep seated fear of people seeing us for who we are. The shame-driven person believes that if anyone knew who they really were, they would not be loved. As a result, if we are shame-based, we feel unlovable unless we are perfect. This is where a refusal to accept responsibility comes in. If we can blame others for our actions, we hope to look faultless and, therefore, better in the eyes of others. Deceiving ourselves into believing that we are less culpable for our actions than we truly are as an attempt to look better in our own eyes can lead to an inflated ego. Instead of understanding that we make mistakes just like everyone else, we tell ourselves that we somehow make less mistakes than everyone else does and are, therefore, better.

In the case of betrayal, it is not uncommon for a certain percentage of wounding partners to blame the wounded partner, at least in part, for their infidelity-related behavior. This is especially common within the first six months of recovery. We want to state in no uncertain terms that **blame toward the wounded partner for any portion of the wounding partner's infidelity-related behavior is entirely inappropriate and highly damaging to both the wounded partner and to the relationship.** We understand that wounded partners have limitations and imperfections as all human beings do. However, when the wounding partner focuses on these limitations and imperfections as a way to blame shift, they are re-wounding their partner in an attempt to make themselves feel better. Infidelity is always a choice. The wounding partner could have dealt with whatever feelings, disappointments, etc. that they were experiencing in a multitude of different ways, and they *chose* to be unfaithful. Even if they were driven by addiction, it was still their choice to not deal with the addiction that led to the infidelity-related behavior. The choice to indulge any behavior at the expense of someone we claim to love is always wrong. This includes infidelity, but can also include blame-shifting, gaslighting, and defensiveness as well.

We get asked by many wounding partners when it is that they can finally talk about the wounded partner's issues instead of theirs. Our answer to that is a challenge. If the wounding partner can go a number of months and take responsibility without defending, then they can check with us to see if it is time to talk about the wounded partner's problems. The length of the challenge varies depending on the individual's propensity to defend and blame. However, generally speaking, the average time is about six months. We don't do this to be mean. Instead, we challenge the wounding partner in this way in order to let the relationship breathe and give the wounded partner time to heal—which cannot happen if blame is constantly being hurled their way. The truth is that a wounded partner is highly unlikely to look at any of their shortcomings until the wounding partner has completely accepted responsibility for their actions without defense for quite some time. When this challenge is completed correctly, it isn't uncommon for the wounded partner to become completely willing to look at other parts of the relationship in order to understand what changes they can personally make to strengthen it. However, it is never appropriate for a wounded partner to accept blame in any way for their partner's choice to betray them. The wounding partner must accept that they are 100% responsible for their actions, and the devastation that those actions have caused if true recovery is to happen within themselves and within the relationship.

Trust-Building Belief #2

"People can change."

The second trust-building belief is that people can change. We want to preface this section by stating that some people *won't* change because they continue to make destructive choices for a myriad of reasons. However, the idea that people *can't* change is an erroneous one. People change all the time. That is not to imply that change comes easily. In the case of mindsets that lead to infidelity and/or addiction, the changes that lead to good relationships with self and others are hard won. They require a vast amount of difficult work in the areas of self-reflection and behavior modification. They also require humility and a willingness to be mentored by someone who has succeeded in the area(s) where success is desired. However, to say that these changes aren't possible just because they aren't easy is entirely false. People do change. How else could we explain the success stories of famous people like Robert Downey Jr. and Jamie Lee Curtis who found their way out of the struggle of substance abuse? Or the countless number of everyday people all over the world who find help for issues such as overeating, sex addiction, and gambling through 12-step programs?

Stanford Professor of Psychology Dr. Carol Dweck has completed multiple studies on students in order to help determine why some people thrive in the face of adversity where others fail. What she discovered is what she refers to as the difference between a growth and a fixed mindset. In her book *Mindset: The New Psychology of Success*, Dr. Dweck attributes the following attitudes to a fixed mindset:

- A focus on validation
- A belief that potential is fixed and pre-determined
- Threatened by the success of others
- A need for certainty
- A reluctance to put in extra effort
- A tendency to crumble under pressure

Whereas those with a growth mindset present the following attitudes:

- A focus on learning
- A desire for ongoing improvement
- A willingness to accept challenges
- A willingness to accept effort as a measure of success
- A willingness to learn from the success of others
- A willingness to learn and grow from failure

In one of her TED Talks, Dr. Dweck makes the statement that the students who had fixed mindsets were "gripped by the tyranny of the now instead of empowered by the 'not yet'". ("Developing a Growth Mindset with Carol Dweck", 2014, TED Talks)

So, how does this apply to recovery from betrayal? The answer is that the belief on both the wounding and the wounded partners' part that change is possible is crucial to the recovery process. If either partner is gripped by the tyranny of the now, it could impede progress that could be made toward the future. When people let go of the idea that abilities are fixed traits, they can open their minds up to the possibility that abilities can, instead, be developed through things like hard work, perseverance, and mentorship. The core belief of a fixed mindset is that everyone has a fixed amount of skills and, therefore, a fixed potential. If someone then fails in a certain area, such as upholding the commitment to be faithful, they have failed altogether and, therefore, do not have what it takes to ever be faithful. This is not necessarily true. Although the phrase, "once a cheater, always a cheater" has some research to back it up, we would submit to you that serial cheaters are such not because of lack of potential, but because of the lack of willingness to do what is necessary to change. People don't engage in infidelity-related behavior because they lack potential. They engage in it because they lack personal and relationship skills and make choices that provide them with what they think of as an easy way out of those challenges. Instead of putting in the hard work necessary to make lasting change, they take what they think is the easier path of self-indulgence and self-gratification.

We encourage wounding partners to take a close look at what might be holding them back from making the changes necessary to help their partner heal and, hopefully, help mend the relationship. If you find yourself resisting change, evaluate your thoughts to see if your resistance could be due to a fixed mindset.

How we respond to the following issues can make the difference between making personal growth and staying stuck:

- Criticism. How we respond to criticism is indicative of our mindset. Those who respond by defending and blaming are typically responding that way because they think if they admit to faults, that makes them less than other people. Instead, try asking yourself if there is any truth to what is being said. If there is, try to make the changes necessary to fix the issue.

- Challenges. When those with a fixed mindset are challenged, they tend to give up almost immediately. Instead of giving up, commit to figuring out what you need to do (not what others need to do) in order to overcome the challenge.

- Setbacks. When those with a fixed mindset encounter a setback, they tend to not only give up but take it as a sign that they don't have what it takes to try again. A growth mindset says that setbacks are valuable learning experiences that can help us do better the next time.

- The skills of others. How we respond to another person being better at something than us says a lot about which mindset we are operating from. Those operating from fixed mindsets will often be threatened by the idea of someone being better than them at something because they think it means that they aren't good enough. Instead of feeling threatened, ask yourself what you can learn from that person in order to increase your own skills.

When we see wounded partners operate from a fixed mindset, it typically shows up as a rigidness toward the wounding partner even if they have truly engaged in recovery. This fixed mindset comes out in statements like, "they will never change" and, "I still don't trust them", even though the wounding partner has been consistent for a significant period of time with recovery work. We would like to qualify this by stating that it is completely normal to have a healthy amount of skepticism about a wounding partner's willingness to change early on in recovery—particularly in the first 6-9 months. In fact, we get concerned when wounded partners extend trust to the wounding partner right away. As we stated previously, trust has to be earned and the wounding partner must show that they are willing to do whatever it takes over an extended period of time to help heal the damage they have caused. Extending trust too quickly, especially without requiring the wounding partner to be ongoingly accountable, is imprudent and could set the wounded partner up for hurt and disappointment later on. Of course it is also possible that the wounding partner is checking "all of the right boxes" of recovery but there has been no change of heart. However, if the couple is well into recovery and the wounding partner has an attitude conducive to rebuilding trust, the wounded partner could be struggling with a fixed mindset.

PART 13

Trust-breaking belief #1

"I am a victim."

Now that we have covered the two most important trust-building beliefs, let's discuss the most common trust-breaking beliefs. When we see these beliefs in our practice, we can accurately predict that both the individual with these beliefs along with the relationship will stall out in recovery.

The first trust-breaking belief is when the wounding partner believes that they are a victim. We all know someone who frequently plays the victim card. The self-pity, the "everything is everyone else's fault", the "poor me". When it comes to working with wounding partners, we often see the victim card played out as blame toward the wounded partner. It can also come out when they seek pity from other members of our coaching groups for what they are having to "endure" at home regarding their partner's anger. We often see it in individual coaching sessions as well; when a wounding partner tries to justify their infidelity-related behavior by talking about how the wounded partner wasn't meeting their needs prior to the affair, to the pornography, or whatever. Some even try to get us to believe that they are the double victim—first of their partner's "neglect", that "made" them act out, and now of their partner's anger toward them because of the betrayal. What they fail to see is that they are the author of their own circumstances.

When wounding partners play the victim card, they try to get everyone around them to accept the fact that they were somehow driven to their infidelity-related behavior out of necessity. They want people to believe that they are somehow faultless victims of cruel partners who neglected them so much that they were driven to cheat, lie, and deceive. That their partner practically forced them to engage in infidelity. When a wounding partner plays the victim card, their sole focus is on image management. They think that by playing the victim that they will somehow look better. That if people will just accept the fact that they were simply being driven to infidelity by valid human needs such as love, attention, sexual intimacy, and affirmation, they will understand how the wounding partner really had no other choice and is, therefore, not to blame for their actions. But they did have a choice, and they chose to betray their partner.

Some wounding partners who play the victim card sound self-righteous. We think this happens because to play the victim, they have to justify their bad behavior in their own mind first. Once the behavior has been justified, they fool themselves into believing that they are somehow the wronged party, and this leads them to self-righteous indignation. The problem is that most of us, especially the wounded partner, aren't buying what they are selling. Playing the victim is unattractive. All it does is highlight to the wounded partner, and almost everyone else, the true depth of that person's self-absorption.

When wounding partners play the victim card, they typically do so out of fear. Many times they want to be rescued or excused from having to do the hard work of recovery because it is daunting due to their lack of skills. The problem is that no one can do the work for another person. While we will admit that the work that needs to be done by the wounding partner in order to rebuild trust in a relationship is difficult, they are the only one who can do it. If they continue to play the victim card instead of doing the work, it makes them unsafe for the wounded partner. The result is often that the wounded partner pulls away in self-protection because they know that, while the wounding partner is busy wallowing in self-pity, they have been completely forgotten.

What wounding partners who play the victim card don't realize is that they are missing a chance to help heal the relationship. By seeing something intimidating like recovery and moving toward it out of a commitment to the relationship, the wounding partner is showing courage which could, over time, win them the respect of the wounded partner. Even if the relationship cannot be restored, the wounding partner still needs to do the work so that they don't carry their issues into a new relationship down the road.

A Word About Resentments

If you are a wounded partner reading this, please don't take what we have to say about the wounding partner's resentments toward you as us condoning their behavior. As we have stated many times, the decision to engage in infidelity-related behavior is 100% the responsibility of the wounding partner. You did nothing to make your partner choose to betray you instead of dealing with issues in a constructive way. That being said, we do need to address the issue of the wounding partner's resentments toward the wounded partner because these resentments often represent justifications in their mind for their behavior and can lead to victim mentality.

When we work with wounding partners, it is not uncommon for them to have resentments that they hold against the wounded partner. While we encourage that all wounding partners take 100% responsibility for their poor choices, we understand that it is unwise to leave these resentments undealt with. Whether the wounding partner has built up resentments out of unrealistic expectations, entitlement, or real issues, they will need to deal with these if recovery is to take place. From our standpoint, it isn't the wounding partner's resentment and anger that are truly the problem. It is the fact that they often use those feelings to justify bad behavior. If you are a wounding partner reading this, it is of utmost importance that you surround yourself with people that do not reinforce your need to justify in any way. You should not share your resentments with your partner within the first six to twelve months of recovery because this will be extremely hurtful to them and come off as blaming. However, if you are a wounding partner with resentments, you will need somewhere safe to work through your feelings. We recommend that you engage a trained coach or counselor in order to work on anger and resentment toward your partner. Your coach or counselor can also help you decide when the right time would be for you to share your issues with your partner, should the need arise. If you hold onto your anger and resentment, you will not only stall out in your own recovery process, but you will likely continue to engage in defending, blaming, and playing the victim, which will further damage your relationship.

Trust-breaking belief #2

"The grass is greener on the other side."

We hear this occasionally from both partners when infidelity has become an issue in their relationship. For the wounding partner, it is often because they are romanticizing their affair partner, the pornography, etc. because it helped them escape from their issues. For the wounded partner, this can look like reminiscing about an old flame, wondering if they should find another relationship, or, even worse, have an affair of their own.

Regardless of your situation, if you are entertaining the idea that the grass is greener somewhere else, we can assure you that it is not.

When wounding partners complain about the grass being greener elsewhere, they are usually trying to justify their actions by explaining how bad their relationship was prior to their engagement in infidelity-related behavior. While all relationships have issues, we often find that the grass wasn't green in the relationship because the wounding partner was failing to water it. If they had invested half of the time, effort, money, and attention in their relationship as they did in their infidelity-related behavior, they would have found that the garden of their relationship would have blossomed from their efforts. Sadly, they were, and still are, so busy indulging the "what ifs" they neglect the "what is". As a result, the grass directly beneath their feet has begun to wither and die.

In the case of sexual or emotional infidelity, it is often the allure of getting instead of giving that trips wounding partners up. When life with their partner becomes hectic or troubled, they feel the urge to escape, and an affair seems to offer all the reward with none of the work. What they fail to understand is that affairs happen outside of the realities of life and that, sooner or later, their troubles will resurface. This is especially true if they end up leaving the wounded partner for an affair partner. As we stated previously, research shows that approximately 75% of marriages based on affairs end in divorce. In the case of the wounding partner who wants to keep their current relationship, they have now increased the magnitude of the relationship's problems a hundredfold.

A Word About Retaliatory Affairs

In our coaching practice, we run across a fair number of wounded partners who entertain thoughts of having an affair or who actually have an affair themselves after they discover that their partner has been unfaithful. Although this isn't particularly surprising, it is concerning to us since we witness the devastation that infidelity causes to individuals and relationships on a daily basis.

When the wounded partner discovers that their partner has been unfaithful, it is one of the most immensely painful events that a person can go through. As a result, it's not surprising that many wounded partners entertain thoughts of getting back at their partner one way or another by having an affair or imagine that their pain would be lessened if they had the distraction of an affair of their own. If you think about it, a "revenge" affair can seem like the perfect way to do that...at least on the surface.

When we hear that someone has had an affair or is entertaining thoughts of one in response to their partner's infidelity-related behavior, it is typically for one of the following four reasons:

1. To hurt their partner as much as they were hurt or "even the score"

2. To teach their partner a lesson

3. To make their partner empathize with or understand the pain they are in

4. To provide themselves with a distraction from the immense pain that they are feeling

Although we certainly understand the reasoning, our experience working with betrayed partners and couples working through betrayal has shown us that the outcome is usually the exact opposite of what the wounded partner had in mind. This is for four main reasons:

> 1. The bond has already been severed. When your partner engaged in their affair or other infidelity-related behavior, one of the reasons it hurt you so badly is because there was an active bond between you and your partner, at least on your side of things. If you engage in a revenge affair, you will be unable to even the score because the impact of your actions won't have nearly the same effect on your partner as they did on you.

> 2. It can make the wounding partner feel better. There's something about human nature that yearns for the scales to be balanced when a wrong has been committed. We have heard wounding partners tell us that knowing their partner did the same thing as they did absolved them of their guilt.

> 3. It can make the wounding partner feel justified. For some wounding partners, especially the unrepentant ones, the fact that their partner engaged in a revenge affair gives them just the excuse they need to carry on with their own bad behavior. For some, this means an excuse to continue their affair or other infidelity-related behavior. For others, it means giving them an excuse to minimize their actions, refuse to accept responsibility, or minimize the wounded partner's feelings.

> 4. It often makes the wounded partner feel bad about themselves. In most cases, the wounded partner is not the one who would normally engage in an affair. If the wounded partner has not cheated up to this point, they probably value their relationship and are concerned with hurting other people. As a result, the wounded partner ends up feeling terrible about themselves because they had to compromise their values in order to engage in their affair.

What makes us sad about these situations is that, if reconciliation is the goal, revenge affairs complicate the process so much that it can take years to untangle all of the issues. The adage "two wrongs don't make a right" definitely applies in this situation. In the case of infidelity, two wrongs only make it worse.

If you are a wounded partner and reconciliation is not your goal or is not possible, we still encourage you to think long and hard before retaliating with an affair of your own. Engagement in a revenge affair can hurt your individual recovery in the following ways:

- The feeling of betrayal doesn't go away, but is now compounded with guilt and shame

- Respect for yourself can go down because you become like the person who betrayed you

- It distracts from emotions and trauma that need to be dealt with

- As mentioned previously, it can cause you to go against your own morals and values

- If you have children, you set a poor example

Affairs and infidelity-related behavior leave a debt that simply can't be repaid. If you are a wounded partner and your partner is willing to do the work, please take some time to decide if you think reconciliation is a possibility before making decisions and, please, don't engage in an affair of your own based on an emotionally charged situation. If, over time, your partner is still "not getting it" or hasn't chosen you, moving on in your life will be much easier without the guilt and shame that can result from retaliation and/or decisions made from pain.

We would also like to mention the "grass is greener" syndrome when it comes to intimacy avoidance and intimacy anorexia®. According the book *Intimacy Anorexia: Healing the Hidden Addiction in Your Marriage*, the author, Dr. Doug Weiss, explains that one of the tactics that intimacy anorexics use in order to maintain distance is "the fantasy person". According to Weiss, the fantasy person is a real or imagined person that the IA keeps in their mind and compares their partner to. This "fantasy person" typically has attributes that the IAs partner does not and, oftentimes, these attributes are completely unattainable for the IAs partner. For example, the IA may be in a relationship with a short person yet talk about how they are attracted to people who are tall. These unfair comparisons to the "fantasy person" provides the IA with an excuse to withdraw from their partner because, in their mind, the partner is faulty. Distance within the relationship happens with the wounded partner, who never feels good enough, withdraws and/or when the IA withdraws in silent judgement. This particular take on the "grass is greener" syndrome deeply damages the wounded partner mentally and emotionally.

Trust Breaking Belief #3

"My partner should complete me."

We blame this one on Hollywood. If you watch any number of movies, you will soon realize that the message being sent is that, somehow, all it takes is the right person to come along and —poof—we will be complete. Whether it is the fairytale princess waiting for her prince to save her, or the bad boy who suddenly changes when he meets the right woman, the message is clear: the pain of life will be cured when we meet the right person.

There are a few problems with this idea, but the main one is that it is completely false. We can never be completed by another person, and we can never complete another person. Our deep-rooted issues and pain do not magically disappear once we find the right relationship. In fact, our shortcomings will often be magnified in our interactions with our partner. The traumatized princess will still have issues even if her prince does come. The Hollywood "bad boy" will not magically cease all his behaviors once in a relationship. He will almost surely repeat them.

When a person believes that their partner should be the be-all, end-all solution to their issues, they are heavily disappointed when this is not the case. This often leads them to become disillusioned and blame their partner for falling short. The truth, however, is that the expectation of their partner meeting their every need and desire was completely unrealistic to begin with. In the case of infidelity, wounding partners often use these unrealistic expectations to justify their actions. This can be reinforced within a culture that overvalues sexuality, which in turn creates entitlement around sex that can lead to ego injury if a person perceives they are being rejected. Additionally, although the wounded partner has every right to expect the wounding partner to be faithful, their pain caused by betrayal cannot be fixed solely by their partner. Although the wounding partner will need to help the recovery process by committing to honesty and transparency without blame or defensiveness moving forward, this will only go partway to healing the wounded partner's pain. The wounded partner will need to take responsibility for their own recovery if complete healing is to occur.

In a 2014 interview for TED Radio entitled *Are We Asking Too Much of Our Spouses?*, renowned psychologist Ether Perel puts it this way:

> *"So we come to one person, and we basically are asking them to give us what once an entire village used to provide.*

Give me belonging, give me identity, give me continuity, but give me transcendence and mystery all in one. Give me comfort. Give me edge. Give me novelty. Give me familiarity. Give me predictability. Give me surprise."

The truth of the matter is that we all need to understand where our responsibilities lie and step up to the plate. This holds true for the wounding partner who justifies their infidelity-related behavior with their partner's real or perceived shortcomings. It also holds true for the wounded partner who refuses to engage in recovery because they are waiting for the wounding partner to fix it all. This last statement is not meant to minimize the fact that the wounding partner has caused many of the issues the wounded partner is now facing. However, regardless of how the wounds came about, the wounded partner is now responsible for doing the work necessary to ensure that they are not permanently damaged from their partner's behavior. Accountability and responsibility for each person's issues is imperative if recovery after betrayal is to take place. This may require one or both parties to adjust their expectations. Relationships should, of course, bring us happiness. However, they are not a fix for our own personal issues.

Trust Breaking Belief #4

"I caused my partner's infidelity."

This last one is not a trust-breaking belief per se. However, it is a belief that can hold the wounded partner back from making progress in their recovery. If we have not been clear up to this point, we never blame the wounded partner for the wounding partner's infidelity-related behavior. The choice to betray is 100% the responsibility of the wounding partner. Thus, the wounded partner shares none of the blame.

If you are a wounded partner reading this, and you feel that your partner's behavior is your fault, we want to help you understand that it isn't. Many wounded partners feel this way because they realize that they haven't been perfect in the relationship. The fact of the matter is that no one is perfect, but that never excuses infidelity. If your conscience is bothering you about something you have done and you want to look at where you might do better in order to improve your relationship, that is commendable. However, owning a facet of how the relationship could be improved is completely different than taking on fault for your partner's infidelity-related behavior.

Many wounded partners start to believe that the betrayal was their fault because the wounding partner overtly or subtly blames them for it. Oftentimes, especially early in recovery, the wounding partner is adamant that the wounded partner should share some of the blame for their infidelity-related behavior. They will often cite the fact that the wounded partner was not meeting their emotional needs, not giving them enough sex, or not being available enough. This can be extremely confusing when the wounding partner believes their own justifications so wholeheartedly that the accusations come off as true. This scenario is especially prevalent in relationships where intimacy avoidance is present. Since gaslighting, blaming, and minimization have been part of the relationship for so long, the wounded partner's mind may be cloudy and confused as to what is actually real. The result is that they may take on blame that isn't theirs to take on.

No relationship is 100% satisfying, and no person is 100% perfect. If those things were valid justifications for infidelity, then everyone would be unfaithful. The truth is that the wounding partner could have dealt with their feelings in a number of ways, and they *chose* infidelity-related behavior as their option. Furthermore, many of the attitudes of a wounding partner are often based in unrealistic expectations and entitlement. These attitudes are based on the wounding partner's flawed way of thinking and, as such, are solely their responsibility to deal with. When a wounding partner blames their partner, they are trying to push off their guilt and the responsibility to change onto the other person so that they don't have to look at themselves. Wounding partners do not engage in infidelity-related behaviors because the wounded partner is faulty. They engaged in infidelity because they *chose* to do so based on a sense of entitlement, self-centeredness, and justifications.

PART 14

Rebuilding Trust Pyramid Layer #2

Safety

Most of the couples that we work with report a lack of safety in their relationship once betrayal has been discovered or disclosed. This feeling of unsafety is especially prevalent for the wounded partner. This makes sense since the agreements that the couple entered the relationship with were violated when the wounding partner engaged in the infidelity-related behavior. Any time a person breaks a promise to their partner, whether that be sexual exclusivity or just making the relationship a priority in their life, it calls the safety of the relationship into question. This is because, for safety to exist, trust must exist. If a person is not true to their word, trust is broken.

When we refer to the word "safety", we are referring to two main types of safety that have been affected by the wounding partner's actions. The primary type of safety that gets affected is what we refer to as emotional safety. When a person is emotionally safe in a relationship, it means that they feel that their emotional experience is cared about and validated. Without emotional safety, a person will have a hard time sharing their fears, dreams, hopes, and pain. In fact, they will be highly unlikely to share anything remotely resembling vulnerability with their partner for fear of being discounted. Betrayal creates emotional unsafety for the wounded partner because, through their actions, the wounding partner showed a complete disregard of how those actions would affect their partner. In the case of the intimacy avoidant relationship, the wounded partner feels a lack of emotional safety at all times because the IAs actions invalidate the wounded partner's emotional experience on a regular basis. In the case of sexual infidelity, the wounded partner's sexual safety is also affected. When the wounding partner goes outside of the relationship, it is not uncommon for them to continue to have sexual relations with the wounded partner as well. This is a complete violation of the wounded partner's body and indicates a profound lack of respect on the wounding partner's part.

All of the couples that we work with are dealing with the unsafety caused by a massive breach of trust due to betrayal. However, as we work with them over time, it becomes apparent in many of the cases that trust has been broken down through other infractions as well. Let's use, for example, the case of childcare. If one partner feels that the other one does not take good care of the children when they are away, this can lead to a frustrating situation in which the responsible partner now feels they have to babysit their partner. Or, if one partner refuses to take ownership over normal chores associated with running the household and the other partner is constantly having to remind them, it wears on the fabric of the relationship over time. This lack of prioritization can result in a breakdown of trust because the partner sees this as a lack of reliability. Other examples could be overspending, poor time management (making someone late all the time) or throwing someone under the bus in order to look good. Once a partner questions another partner's reliability, trust becomes fragile. If enough infractions happen over time, the result is broken trust.

Perhaps the best example of this phenomenon can be seen in the intimacy avoidant relationship. In the case of intimacy avoidance, the IA's actions are considered to be unfaithful because they have chosen to put themselves first. In the intimacy avoidant relationship, there can certainly be sexual infidelity, emotional infidelity, and infidelity through pornography. However, even if these things aren't present, trust is almost always missing. This is because the IA uses multiple ways to withhold from their partner in order to create an imbalance of power in their own favor. They then use minimization, defensiveness, and gaslighting to keep the wounded partner from gaining equal footing in the relationship. This combination, often present even at the beginning of the relationship, causes a situation in which trust cannot be fostered. One common example of this is when the IA overworks or acts too preoccupied to pay real attention to their partner. When the partner brings this up, their feelings are usually minimized with statements such as, "you're being overly sensitive." Or worse, they are gaslighted and told that the IA does, in fact, make plenty of time for them. This creates a void of safety. As opposed to the abrupt break in safety that we see in other types of betrayal, in many cases, almost every area of the intimacy avoidant relationship feels unsafe to the wounded partner.

When we address the subject of safety with the couples we work with, we typically talk about it in two parts. The first part of safety is built through a commitment to recovery and the attitudes and demeanor of both parties in the relationship. Additionally, the first stage of building safety requires that we work with a couple to outline the actual plans that need to be put into place that address that relationship's particular issues. We will be covering those things in this section. The second part of safety is built through consistently working the plans put in place, the wounding partner consistently being accountable for their time and whereabouts, and, again, consistency in showing a demeanor conducive to the rebuilding of trust. This is applicable to both parties in the relationship but is especially applicable to the wounding partner. We will cover this important part of building and maintaining safety in the next section on consistency.

Demeanor

Until the wounded partner feels a great deal of safety within the relationship, little-to-no progress will be made toward rebuilding trust. One of the main ways that safety can begin to be reestablished—or established for the first time in the case of the intimacy avoidant relationship— is through the demeanor of the wounding partner. If the wounding partner continues to be resistant to recovery or acts prideful, defensive, and/or arrogant, the wounded partner will not feel safe enough to engage in the recovery of the relationship. It is not enough to end the infidelity-related behavior, although this is extremely important. The wounding partner needs to be able to show true remorse for their actions. Arrogance, pride, and defensiveness send the wounded partner the message that the wounding partner is not truly sorry for what they have done and/or does not understand the effect that their actions have had on their partner.

When a wounding partner engages in infidelity-related behavior, they selfishly set the wounded partner aside in favor of something else. As a result, the wounded partner feels disrespected, unimportant, and forgotten. This is why it is of the utmost importance that the wounding partner show that they will do whatever it takes to win their partner back. If the wounding partner continues to display a lack of humility by acting defensive, arrogant, or prideful, the message that is inadvertently conveyed to the wounded partner is that they should not ask for what they need in order to heal. Instead, they should just be happy with whatever the wounding partner is willing to give. A defensive, prideful, or arrogant demeanor on the wounding partner's part sends the message that they do not value their partner. Someone with this type of demeanor needs to ask themselves why anyone would want to stay with someone who shows them this type of disrespect. Why should anyone stay with a person who could cast them aside in an act of unfaithfulness and then continue to act remorseless about it and/or protect their own self-interest?

When we view things in this light, we begin to understand how gracious the wounded partner is being by offering the wounding partner another chance. This chance is a gift of high value and should be taken very seriously by the wounding partner. If the wounding partner casts it aside in the interest of their own pride and comfort, it is highly unlikely that they are truly sorry for their behavior or understand the effects of their actions.

If you are a wounding partner reading this and your partner is continuing to emotionally flood, chances are that you are engaging in behavior that is causing them to feel unsafe. If you cannot or will not do everything you can to create a safe environment for your partner, any advances toward the restoration of the relationship will be slow to non-existent. If you do not know what it is that you need to do, you should ask your partner at a time when they are not emotionally flooded. Typically, the things that make a wounded partner feel most safe are prioritization of the relationship, accountability for your actions and whereabouts, your availability to listen to them and meet their needs, and the consistency at which you behave in a manner that they interpret as loving. However, your partner may have other requirements. If these requirements are reasonable, agree to meet them. If you are not sure if they are reasonable, engage the help of a trained professional to help you understand.

As the wounding partner, earning back trust will require a great deal of patience on your part. You may tell your partner time and time again that you are "all in", but it takes much more than words to prove to them that you mean it. Rushing your partner toward "recovery" by complaining about their need to talk about it or shutting them down is not only unfair and inappropriate, but it comes across as controlling and uncaring. You need to remember that their reactions are in response to your deception. It is going to take quite a while before they believe that you are no longer engaged in a double life. A word of caution: we see many wounding partners, especially intimacy avoidants, insist that their partner stop bringing the up betrayal in conversation. This will backfire if you are at all interested in the restoration of trust in the relationship. Wounded partners who are shut down in this way share with us that they continue to feel a profound lack of trust and safety, even if they aren't voicing it. The only thing that shutting the conversation down does is ensure that the wounded partner does not share their feelings with you. This erodes trust even further over the long run and often results in the relationship ending.

Ambivalence

Ambivalence is the state of having mixed feelings or contradictory ideas about someone or something. (Oxford Languages) Ambivalence on the part of either partner creates a lack of safety in the relationship. This is because, in order to work on the relationship, both partners need to be committed to doing the work. Notice that we did not say that both partners must know for certain that recovery for the relationship is possible. For many couples, it is normal for one or both parties to not know if the relationship will recover or if reconciliation is truly even what they want. However, a commitment to doing the work necessary to see if the relationship can survive is vital to creating enough safety to move forward with recovery work. If one or both partners remain frozen in inaction due to ambivalence, recovery will stall out.

Ambivalence, although a normal part of the rebuilding trust process for many people, is often painful experience—especially to the wounded partner. Ambivalence on the part of a wounding partner is often excruciating for the wounded partner because it is like pouring salt into a cut. It was hard enough finding out about their partner's betrayal, but to watch the wounding partner vacillate between wanting to stay in the relationship and wanting to leave it is almost unbearable. For the wounding partner with empathy, it can be a hard situation to be in. They don't want to further injure their partner, but they can't help how they feel. It can also be hard for a wounded partner to feel ambivalent about their relationship, especially if the wounding partner is truly sorry for their actions. Unless the wounded partner is using ambivalence to gain back power in the relationship, it doesn't feel good to hurt the wounding partner even though they were hurt themselves by the betrayal.

If you are a wounding or wounded partner who is trying to elicit pain from your partner by acting ambivalent, we urge you to stop. If you are using ambivalence to manipulate the other person, it will do nothing but damage to your already-damaged relationship. For most people, however, ambivalence is an unwelcome feeling. It is often frightening because many people take the presence of ambivalence as a sign that the relationship is doomed. Although prolonged ambivalence on the part of either partner stalls recovery which can ultimately lead to the relationship's demise, we want to tell you that, when handled correctly, it doesn't have to end in separation.

If you are feeling ambivalent about your relationship, it is important that you deal with this feeling head on. If you run from it, it will only prolong the recovery process and could end up backfiring. We realize that it might be scary for you to admit to feelings of ambivalence. However, ignoring your feelings will not make them go away. To quote Dr. Phil McGraw, *"you can't change what you don't acknowledge."* A word of caution: you will need some help dealing with ambivalence. If you had the answers within yourself, you would have come to a decision by now. We recommend enlisting the help of a trained professional in order to help you sift through the intense feelings that create ambivalence. Feelings of ambivalence create an opportunity for a person to truly look at why they want to stay and why they want to leave.

We recommend making a pro's and con's list that includes the consequences of either choice—not only to the partners involved in the relationship, but to children (if any), friends, and family members as well.

We also recommend that you do not make any decisions in your ambivalent state. Instead, we recommend that you set a date in the near future (no more than twelve months) and work diligently toward it. When we say work diligently toward it, we mean embrace the work that you need to do in order to do recovery. If you don't, you are likely to remain in your ambivalent state for an extended period. You don't have to decide about the entire future of the relationship now. Of course, you will have to eventually decide. However, for now, we encourage you to make a choice about working as hard as you can on recovery. This includes engaging, on a frequent basis, the professional help that you enlist to deal with your ambivalence. There is a lot at stake here, and that should not be taken lightly. Commit to working on recovery with your partner in order to see whether the relationship can be saved. The only way out of ambivalence is through it.

If you are a wounded partner dealing with prolonged ambivalence on the part of the wounding partner, it may be time to evaluate your response to the situation. For example, a common tactic of a partner that wants the relationship to work is for them to try to reason with, beg, and even threaten the ambivalent partner into action. Most of the time, this pushes the ambivalent partner further away. It also creates a situation in which the "chaser" gives away their power to the "chasee" every time they chase them. If you are a partner experiencing this, we suggest that you pull back from the situation and possibly put some boundaries in place. We aren't suggesting this tactic as a way to manipulate the ambivalent partner into making the decision to stay in the relationship. Instead, we recommend the "hands-off" approach for the following reasons:

1. **It is empowering.** There is nothing more defeating than chasing someone around who acts like they don't want you. Although it can be painful to accept the reality that your partner may not want to stay, accepting the truth can empower you to make decisions based on the situation you are currently facing.

2. **It conserves emotional energy.** Chasing an ambivalent partner around takes emotional energy from the partner that they can't spare. This energy would be better used if the partner put it toward their own recovery instead.

3. **It helps stop the insanity.** Chasing an ambivalent partner is crazy-making and painful. This can be especially infuriating if the ambivalent partner is the one who was unfaithful. Taking a hands-off approach can help stop the insanity.

If things are going to change, the non-ambivalent partner needs to stop doing the things that are leading them nowhere. When we work with couples, we often find that the dynamics in the relationship before the betrayal were similar to the way they are afterwards. This is to say that it is not uncommon for one of the partners to traditionally be the "chaser" and the other one to be the "chasee". If either partner wants things to change, one or both are going to have to stop doing things the way they have always done them. In this case, the ambivalent partner is unlikely to enact the change. This leaves it up to the non-ambivalent partner to put a stop to the situation. The ambivalent partner is blind to the need for change because their ambivalence has them frozen. When the non-ambivalent partner pulls back, it often creates an urgency for the ambivalent partner to act.

We want to stress that pulling back does not guarantee that the ambivalent partner will make a decision in favor of the relationship. However, chasing them around will surely push them away. If the non-ambivalent partner pulls away and the ambivalent partner does not respond within a few months of the new situation, it may be time for the non-ambivalent partner to put a boundary in place until the ambivalent partner commits to making a choice. Common boundaries in this scenario include separation and even divorce if the partners are married. We recommend that the boundary be time-bound and be stated using one of the two methods shared regarding boundaries in the previous section on honesty.

PART 15

Wounded Partner Pitfalls Pitfall #1

Telling too many people

For this next section, we would like to highlight some common pitfalls that wounded and wounding partners can fall into both individually and as a couple. These pitfalls erode safety within the relationship and make it nearly impossible for recovery to gain any traction. We will start by outlining five common pitfalls wounded partners experience.

Although it can be tempting for the wounded partner to tell whoever they want to about the pain their partner has caused them, we don't recommend it. We have worked with many wounded partners who regularly tell us that they regret telling so many people about their partner's infidelity-related behavior. Telling the wrong people can destroy relationships, damage children, and damage the wounding partner. It is often counterproductive to the recovery of the relationship as well.

Although it is not uncommon for wounded partners not to care who they tell in the beginning because they are determined to leave the relationship, it is our experience that many of them change their mind once some time goes by. This can lead to a situation that the wounded partner comes to regret. One extreme example of this is when a woman we worked with got her husband fired from his job because she wanted to punish him. She later came to regret that decision and realized that she had shot holes in her own boat by doing so.

Although telling a large number of people is not advisable, we don't recommend that wounded partners go it alone either. It is not a healthy situation for the wounded partner to process all their emotions with the wounding partner. We recommend that both the wounding and the wounded partners identify two or three people each that they are going to lean on for support during this time. It is best if both partners can agree on each other's lists so that neither feels betrayed through the sharing of information. However, we understand that sometimes this isn't possible. The purpose of identifying support people ahead of time is that it reduces the likelihood that one or both partners will share with random people out of pain. Sharing the pain of betrayal randomly is not advisable since a person may inadvertently tell someone who will give them bad advice, gossip about their situation, or leave them abandoned in their pain because they don't know how to respond. Hurtful gossip as a result of sharing the pain from betrayal with the wrong person can set an already-fragile relationship up for more damage.

The wounded partner should be careful not to share their experience out of bad motives. Here are some questions to ask when deciding when to share emotions and with whom:

- Am I trying to punish my partner?

- Am I trying to manipulate my partner or the outcome of the relationship?

- Am I feeling self-righteous by sharing this information?

- Will sharing this information serve a positive benefit?

If the wounded partner takes the time to ask themselves these questions before sharing and will limit the number of people they share with, they are likely to save themselves a lot of trouble down the road.

Pitfall #2

Not dealing with underlying issues

We want to preface this by stating that we are not implying that a wounded partner should take on any responsibility for the wounding partner's behavior. The choice to engage in infidelity-related behavior is 100% the responsibility of the wounding partner. That being said, we have seen many wounded partners create a lack of safety in the recovery process by continuing to lash out at their partner through raging, humiliation, threatening, and shaming. Although it is normal for a wounded partner to engage in some of these behaviors (especially within the first three months of disclosure or discovery), a continuous and/or prolonged engagement in these behaviors is an indication that something is going on underneath the pain.

Trauma from betrayal affects multiple areas of a wounded partner's life. It has a way of bringing up past painful experiences as well. Here are some common areas of underlying issues:

- Self-worth
- Control
- Past traumatic events and abuse
- Depression or anxiety
- Co-dependency
- Abandonment

Healing from trauma happens in stages. Thus, it is not uncommon for new trauma to trigger feelings from past trauma and emotional pain. The underlying issues that betrayal brings up are signals that the wounded partner may have unresolved issues and/or needs to go deeper into recovery. This can be frustrating for the wounded partner, who is already dealing with so much. It can be especially frustrating when the wounded partner is being plagued with past issues that they thought were already resolved. Our goal in sharing this information is not to discourage you, but to help prepare you. Dealing with past issues is a normal part of the recovery process.

Pitfall #3

Not enforcing boundaries

Boundaries are an important part of the recovery process for wounded partners. Much of the anger that results from betrayal is because the wounding partner has crossed so many boundary lines. Because boundaries keep us and others safe, a lack of boundary enforcement can lead to an unsafe situation for the wounded partner and for the relationship overall.

We often see wounded partners start out with firm boundaries, only to move their boundary lines when they meet with resistance from the wounding partner or when things start to go better in the relationship. One example of this is when the wounding partner won't honor communication boundaries and continues to rage, hurl insults, threaten, or refuses to honor constraints on the length of time conversations around the betrayal should last. Another example of this is when the wounded partner lets go of insisting on the wounding partner's need to be ongoingly accountable. We will cover both of these issues later. For now, we want to stress that not enforcing boundaries and/or getting lax on boundaries is a mistake.

Sometimes wounded partners let go of their boundaries in an attempt to let go of the past and move on. While it is understandable that neither partner wants to live in the aftermath of betrayal forever, letting go of boundaries is not the way to achieve lasting recovery. In fact, the opposite is true. Boundaries are vital to any healthy relationship. They help others understand how we want to be respected, help us gain a strong sense of identity, and bring focus and attention to our own well-being. A lack of boundaries creates a lack of safety and can cause us to build up some hefty resentments that can eventually lead to the demise of our relationships.

Pitfall #4

Over responsibility

We feel that this one falls into the category of boundaries. However, we see it so often that we think it deserves a section of its own. Although we sometimes see this in both partners, we most often see it in the wounded partner—especially when the wounding partner is ambivalent and/or does not seem to be taking recovery seriously. Due to how significant the effects of betrayal are, it is no wonder that over responsibility would show up. If the wounding partner fails to do the work necessary for the relationship to heal, it can create a situation that feels quite frightening to the wounded partner because there is so much on the line.

The term "over responsibility" can be described as a situation in which a person manages another person in such a way that they take on the responsibility for that person's choices and behaviors. Typically, this situation happens because the over responsible person wants to minimize or avoid pain—particularly rejection, disappointment, and loss. In the case of wounded partners, it often comes across as them "babysitting" the recovery process. They frequently check in with their partner and offer reminders in the form of questions such as, "are you doing the reading?", "did you make that appointment yet?", or "you do realize that your group starts in 15 minutes, right?"

We are not unsympathetic to the wounded partner's pain and acknowledge that it may be the cause of much of over responsible behavior. However, it typically backfires in the following ways:

- The wounded partner continues to feel unsafe because they are unsure of the wounding partner's motives for recovery.

- They never give the wounding partner the opportunity to own their own recovery.

- They use up emotional energy that they can't spare, which can lead to being overwhelmed in multiple areas of life.

- One or both of the partners become resentful.

Although it can be tempting for the wounded partner to engage in behavior that is over responsible, it most often creates frustration for them. It is also important to note that, although managing the wounding partner's recovery process can be tempting and even seem necessary, it is of utmost importance that the wounding partner own the recovery for themselves. They can't be forced into it. If they are, it typically will not last. This can be very difficult for the wounded partner to face, but it's true. If the wounded partner continues to have to do all of the work for recovery, the question is whether or not the wounding partner is really committed in the first place. Conversely, if the wounding partner is simply slow to get going on recovery, over responsibility on the wounded partner's part could push them in the opposite direction.

So what can an over-responsible person do to help the situation? Although overcoming over responsibility is often a long process, especially if the tendency to be over responsible was present prior to the betrayal, here are some things that can help:

- **Own it.** The first step to overcoming an obstacle like over responsibility is to acknowledge that it is an issue.

- **Dig deeper.** Oftentimes, there are deeper issues driving over responsibility that a person needs to discover and work on if they are to stop engaging in this behavior. Common areas include pain, worry, pride, fear, and childhood issues.

- **Self-care.** For many wounded partners, the thought of not being over responsible for their partner's recovery is stressful. It can be nerve wracking to pull back and wait to see if the wounding partner is going to take responsibility for their own recovery. Self-care is critical to help combat this potentially stressful situation.

- **Accountability.** For some, pulling back and taking a "wait and see" attitude when it comes to the wounding partner's recovery is extremely difficult. It can help to put accountability in place so that the wounded partner does not feel tempted to reengage in over responsibility.

- **Self-compassion.** The stakes are high when it comes to recovery from betrayal. Wounding partners should be patient with themselves during this difficult process. If you reengage in the over responsible behavior, get back on track by admitting to it and offer yourself compassion.

Pitfall #5

Going on the attack after the wounding partner shares information

This is a tough one for many wounded partners. On the one hand, the wounded partner desperately needs to understand what their partner has done in order to process the information. On the other hand, they typically feel extremely angry and hurt when they find the information out. This can lead many wounded partners to attack the wounding partner. Although it is completely understandable why the wounded partner would do this, it is counterproductive to recovery and creates a lack of safety in the relationship.

For some wounded partners, the information shared with them can cause such great pain that they lash out physically against their partners. For others, they engage in verbal assaults. As we said, this is understandable but counterproductive. As hard as it may be to accept, the wounded partner needs to provide a safe space for the wounding partner to share information regarding their infidelity-related behavior. If they don't, the wounding partner is likely to withhold information which will stall recovery. We feel it important to say that we never advocate for the wounding partner to hold back information just because this is happening. As we have said previously, the wounding partner needs to be forthcoming with information regarding infidelity-related behavior regardless of the circumstances.

We want anyone reading this to understand that we are not saying that the wounded partner shouldn't be angry or express anger. However, expressing anger, disappointment, hurt, disgust, etc. in an appropriate way is of the utmost importance if the wounded partner wants the dialogue between them and their partner to continue. Name calling, threatening, physically attacking, or throwing things at the wounding partner will create a lack of safety in the relationship. Although it is understandable that the wounded partner would be angry and hurt by the wounding partner's actions, they must work hard at keeping that anger in check. Time outs, which we will cover at length later on in this section, are a good way to ensure that displays of anger are kept at appropriate levels.

If you are a wounded partner and have been in the habit of doing this, you may be facing a situation in which your partner is hesitant or refuses to give you the information you need regarding their infidelity-related behavior. In order to reestablish safe communication, we would advise you to commit to not reacting to the information your partner gives you right away. Instead, we recommend that you commit to not acting on the information for a certain period of time after you have received it. Depending on the circumstances and the type of information received, this could be anything from 24 hours to one year participating in a couple's recovery program.

PART 16

Wounding Partner Pitfalls

Since we have already explained the major mistakes of not ending the infidelity-related behavior and defending and blaming, we will not detail those here. Instead, we would like to offer you information on other common mistakes that wounding partners make that sabotage safety in the recovery process.

Pitfall #1: Lying (about anything)

It goes without saying that the wounding partner should never lie about what their infidelity-related behavior entails. However, it is also important to remember that lying about anything will leave the wounded partner wondering if there is any hope for safety in the relationship.

According to Merriam-Webster, the definitions of lying best suited to the purposes of this book are as follows:

1. To make an untrue statement with the intent to deceive

2. To create a false and/or misleading impression

There are three common types of lies that people tell. These are:

1. Lies of commission. Lying by intentionally using false statements.

2. Lies of omission. Lying by failing to disclose relevant information.

3. Lies of influence (a.k.a. "character lies"). Lying by not directly answering the question but, instead, offering a statement about your character that implies that you would never do such a thing.

When a couple is working through the aftermath of betrayal, even seemingly innocuous lies are a huge deal to the wounded partner. Because the wounding partner engaged in deception when they engaged in their infidelity-related behavior, every lie told from here on out could constitute a reason why the wounded partner feels they cannot trust the wounding partner. This includes "white lies" and leaving out seemingly unimportant details.

Pitfall #2: Checking boxes

When we work with wounded partners who feel unsafe in the relationship, we are often told that this is because they feel that the wounding partner is simply "checking boxes" when it comes to recovery. What they mean by this is that the wounding partner is only going through the motions when it comes to their recovery work, but there has been very little change in their demeanor and attitudes. If you are a wounding partner reading this and this describes your situation, we challenge you to dig deep within yourself in order to discover why. If it is because of ambivalence on your part, we encourage you to deal with that head-on. Until you do, your relationship will stall out in terms of recovery.

It is important for the wounding partner to understand that the wounded partner is not interested in having items on a list checked off—especially if it is only being done to placate them or to make the wounding partner look good. What the wounded partner is looking for from the wounding partner are signs of a change of heart. If the wounding partner is disengaged from the process of true recovery, it sends the message to the wounded partner that the relationship is not a priority.

Here are some common ways that wounding partners come across as if they are merely "checking boxes":

- Getting information but failing to apply it to their actions.

- Setting themselves up as the exception to the rule when it comes to what they should be doing.

- Making the wounded partner do all of the work when it comes to making counseling/coaching appointments, finding self-help books to read, etc.

- Making their recovery work dependent on their partner changing.

Pitfall #3: A lack of humility

"Pride makes us artificial, and humility makes us real."— Thomas Merton

When couples are trying to recover from the effects of betrayal, a lack of humility on the wounding partner's part creates a lack of safety in the relationship that brings recovery to a grinding halt. When we work with wounding partners who lack humility, we often feel like we are talking to a brick wall. It is unfortunate because their pride keeps them from benefitting from the information that is vital to both their personal recovery and the recovery of the relationship.

Here are some signs that pride is an issue:

- Being defensive
- Being argumentative
- Talking over the top of people
- A focus on being heard instead of hearing other people
- Excuse-making
- Hiding flaws
- Blaming

When wounding partners lack humility, they are unsafe. They put themselves and their relationship in danger because the wounded partner will feel that they can't freely talk about the issues that would help them recover. And the wounded partner isn't the only one who suffers. Wounding partners who lack humility set themselves up for future failure because they don't understand their ability to engage in infidelity-related behavior in the future. Instead, they often tell themselves that they will never do it again because their pride clouds their understanding of their own vulnerability. Additionally, wounding partners who lack humility cut themselves off from a community of people who could help them with the issues they are dealing with.

Pitfall #4: Expecting the wounded partner to "just get over it"

Although it can seem like it would be beneficial for the relationship to have everyone, particularly the wounded partner, move on, dismissing the gravity of the situation with a quick fix is a mistake of huge proportions. If you are a wounding partner reading this, and you are interested in saving your relationship, we cannot stress enough the fact that you should immediately stop. When you engage in this type of behavior, you marginalize your because an attitude of "just get over it" implies that the issue is not as big of a deal as they are making it out to be. If you continue to marginalize your partner in this way, you are acting disrespectfully and risk pushing them away from you completely and permanently.

Here are a few of the statements that wounding partners make that marginalize wounded partners:

- "Why can't we just move on?"
- "It meant nothing to me. I don't see what the big deal is."
- "When are you going to stop bringing this up?"
- "I said I was sorry. You need to forgive me."
- "Haven't we talked about this enough already?"
- "I don't see why you're still upset."

Unfortunately, we hear these types of statements in our offices on a regular basis. The dismissive attitude that typically accompanies these statements is not only harmful to the wounded partner, but it can also create huge barriers to the recovery of the relationship. Additionally, it can be an indication of denial on the wounding partner's part. Instead of choosing to look at the evidence that suggests that their infidelity-related behavior was, in fact, a VERY big deal, they choose to believe that it wasn't. However, denying the truth does not change the facts of the situation. The wounded partner is doing and saying the things they are because the infidelity-related behavior was extremely damaging, violating, and world-changing. The wounded partner's pain should be all the evidence the wounding partner needs to acknowledge that their betrayal was, and is, a big deal.

Another take on the "just get over it" situation is when we see the wounding partner engage in recovery and expect that this is enough to fix the wounded partner's pain. If you are a wounding partner reading this, we would remind you that individual recovery, while great for everyone involved, is not enough to immediately fix the situation. This is especially true for wounding partners involved in pornography addiction, sex addiction, and/or intimacy avoidant behavior. In our programs, people working the 12-steps for these issues often get a sobriety date. While this is fantastic, and we want to commend those of you entering into sobriety on their efforts, you need to understand that your sobriety date is likely a painful reminder to your partner of the date that you last acted out. As such, they are highly unlikely to feel the same sense of pride about it as you do.

What is important for wounding partners to remember is that they should not expect a large amount of praise from the wounded partner for good behavior, or simply for a lack of bad behavior. Expecting praise for behaving better than when they were acting out is a lot like expecting praise for not hitting the wounded partner in the head with a hammer. While it is great that they aren't hitting them in the head with a hammer anymore, the fact remains that they once did hit them in the head with the "hammer" of infidelity-related behavior. Expecting them to be overly grateful for this is unrealistic. While we understand that recovery is difficult and encouragement is often helpful to sustained self-improvement, we encourage wounding partners to remember that expecting praise for a *lack of bad behavior* is not only unrealistic but can come off as self-serving and unempathetic. Instead, it is better for the wounding partner to join a workgroup such as the ones we offer at Becoming Well in order to gain insight and encouragement from other group members.

In recovery, we use the term "pink clouding" to describe a situation in which the wounding partner feels excited about their own recovery. Pink clouding is most common when the wounding partner has been engaged in addictive behavior and is marked by the following:

- Feelings of joy and/or excitement
- A hopeful outlook
- Optimism
- Confidence
- Calmness
- A heavy focus on recovery-related behaviors
- Commitment to change
- A tendency to overlook the hard work needed to maintain recovery
- Increased awareness of their own emotions

While pink clouding offers a much-needed shift of focus, it can be difficult for the wounded partner to see the wounding partner respond this way. We have been told by many wounded partners that they often feel jealous of the wounding partner's ability to feel optimistic and joyful because the situation is quite different for them. For a wounded partner who has experienced betrayal, they are left struggling through the aftermath of shattered hopes and dreams. Feelings of comfort and safety are gone, and the wounded partner is left staring into the unknown. This often leaves the wounded partner with a bleak sense of hopelessness that they will have to work through if they are to feel joy within the relationship once more. If you are a wounding partner reading this and are pink clouding, we advise you to keep this in mind. Although it is wonderful that you have fully engaged in recovery, and we don't want to discourage you from that, we want to encourage you to balance out the excitement you feel at your own recovery with the perspective that your partner is likely struggling. Please do not adopt the attitude that they should "just get over it" and come along in recovery with you. Instead, acknowledge that their path is different than yours and commit to listening to, empathizing with, and acknowledging their pain, because it is pain that you created for them.

Pitfall #5: Not supporting the wounded partner's recovery

If you are a wounding partner reading this, we need to stress that it is important that you support your partner's individual recovery. In our work with wounding partners, we have discovered that a certain percentage of them seem to have trouble with this concept for the following reasons:

- It embarrasses them to have their secrets revealed to other people. While we understand that it can be embarrassing for the wounding partner to have someone else know what they have done, it is important that this is dealt with as a separate issue and not projected onto the wounded partner. It is important to the wounded partner's recovery that they have people to process emotions with who will give them sound advice and caring support. If this is an issue, we urge you to deal with it in order to resolve the issue for yourself. Putting your own comfort before the well-being of your partner sends the message that you aren't prioritizing the relationship.

- It costs them money. Yes, recovery can be expensive—especially recovery from betrayal because the process takes a long time. We understand that not everyone is financially able to engage in every single experience that would help them recover. However, the wounding partner needs to make recovery for both themselves and the wounded partner a priority. Our advice is for the wounding partner to prioritize spending on recovery-related activities.

- The wounded partner's autonomy threatens them. Unfortunately, we see this on a regular basis—especially in relationships where intimacy avoidance is an issue. Some relationships are defined by the wounding partner's need to control the wounded partner's autonomy in order to avoid abandonment and/or rejection. For others, it can be scary because they know their infidelity-related behavior may cause their partner to leave them. If you are feeling threatened by your partner's autonomy in this situation, we urge you to deal with this as a separate issue.

- They want to minimize the problem. Sadly, some wounding partners care more about looking bad than they do about their partner's recovery. Minimizing in any way is self-serving and will hurt the wounded partner and the relationship. We urge wounding partners who minimize to stop putting themselves and their feelings above the needs of their partner to heal.

- They do not consider their partner's needs to be important or as important as theirs. We see this occasionally in intimacy avoidant and narcissistic relationships. For some wounding partners, their needs, feelings, desires, etc. come before anyone else's and especially before the wounded partner's. The root of this issue is usually a fragile sense of self-worth. Many wounding partners who feel this way actually feel bad about themselves and mistakenly think that acknowledging the importance of someone else's needs somehow diminishes their own importance.

As we stated previously, it is imperative that the wounded partner get their own individual recovery after betrayal has been discovered or disclosed. Supporting their recovery is a way that the wounding partner can show remorse for their actions as well as love toward the wounded partner.

PART 17

Pitfalls As a Couple

Pitfall #1: Failing to prioritize ongoing accountability

One of the biggest mistakes a couple can make in recovery is for one or both of partners to fail making accountability a priority. Typically, we see this happen for one of the following reasons:

1. The wounding partner is being lax with recovery.

2. The wounded partner gets tired of pushback when they ask for accountability.

3. The wounded partner fails to understand ways in which they themselves need to be accountable.

4. One or both partners feel the relationship has improved so much that accountability is no longer needed.

Reasons one and two indicate that there is a lack of true recovery on the wounding partner's part. This is problematic because, if true recovery does not take place, the relationship is not a safe place because the infidelity-related behavior has a high likelihood of resurfacing at some point. As for reason number three, it isn't uncommon for wounded partners to feel that it is their partner that needs recovery—not them. One of our goals in working with wounded partners is to help them understand that they need their own recovery due to the fact that experiencing trauma from betrayal is like being hit by a bus. Although it was through no fault of their own, they will still need to heal and recover from their injuries. Additionally, the wounded partner will need ongoing accountability for any behaviors they are engaging in that hurt the relationship.

Reason number four is, perhaps, the most dangerous reason for not prioritizing ongoing accountability because it is the hardest one to explain to couples who are finally doing better. Most couples who have struggled through infidelity and come out the other side just want to put everything behind them and move on. While this is certainly understandable, we would like to point out that there is a difference between talking about the betrayal all of the time (which is not recommended) and keeping good recovery habits in place.

Oftentimes, wounding partners have every intention of holding true to their promises. Unfortunately, it is one thing for a person to say that they would never do something again and another to keep the necessary guardrails in place to keep them from running off the track. When it comes to recovery from betrayal, especially when addiction is in the mix, good intensions simply aren't enough. Habits, especially ones related to infidelity-related behavior, are like ruts in the road of life. It only takes a person getting a little bit off track before they realize that their wheels have slipped into those ruts, and they are now following an all-too-familiar path to destruction.

As human beings, when we travel down a good road for a long period of time it is easy for us to forget about the ruts in the road that lead down a bad path. We can tell ourselves that we aren't the same person we used to be, that we can bend the rules and still be fine, or that we are so far away from the ruts that lead to the bad path that there is no way we could ever go back there again. Unfortunately, life doesn't work like that. It is a journey, not a destination. To think that we have arrived is to set ourselves up for possible relapse.

What we recommend is that each partner outline the behaviors that are non-optional, the behaviors that are life-giving, and the questionable, or "slippery", behaviors. Each person should do this for themselves, although it can be a good couple's exercise to do as well. An easy way to outline these behaviors is to use a 3-Circle Exercise:

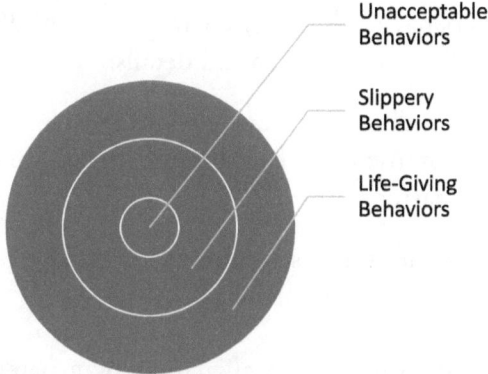

Figure 3: 3-Circle Exercise

Next, outline the accountability you are going to put into place in order to sustain each one. Although this exercise can be somewhat time consuming, it is highly valuable because it can help the relationship, and the individuals in it, to stay on track. Taking a proactive approach to accountability is vital to recovery. We have known many people who have done well in recovery for years who seem to suddenly slip off the rails due to stressors in their life. What we discover is that most of them gave up on the daily routine of accountability long before they acted out. As opposed to simply reacting when things get hard, proactively engaging in ongoing accountability will help ensure that the necessary guardrails are in place if and when times get stressful.

Pitfall #2: Using children as pawns

Unfortunately, this is common enough that we had to include it in this book. When one parent bad-mouths another parent, can create a harmful situation for the child(ren) involved. Although most parents we work with understand why it is not in their children's best interest to do this, we occasionally run across it in the following scenarios:

1. The wounded partner is so disgusted with the wounding partner's behavior that they try to get the child(ren) on their side by telling them the sordid details.

2. The wounding partner, not wanting to look bad, gets the child(ren) on their side by telling them bad things about the wounded partner.

3. One partner purposely hurts their child(ren) as a way to get back at the other partner.

Studies have shown that alienation by a parent can create mental health, relationship, self-esteem, trust, anger, substance abuse, and learning issues for children. Although it is only human to want the empathy of others during this difficult time, we implore you to leave your child(ren) out of it. Additionally, we do not recommend that either partner use even their older child(ren) as confidantes, although it is okay to tell them the truth. Please keep in mind that the details given need to be age appropriate. For example, telling a young child that the wounding partner did not treat the wounded partner in a loving way is truthful, but still age appropriate. It is okay to tell a grown child more details such as, "Mom had an affair". However, we still recommend that you err on giving children, no matter what age, as little detail as possible and not involve them in what is going on.

Pitfall #3: Marathon conversations

A marathon conversation is a conversation that should take 45 minutes or less to discuss but ends up turning into a conversation that lasts for hours, and even days. We've had couples report that some discussion marathons have lasted all night into the wee hours of the morning, rendering both parties exhausted and barely able to function during the daytime. Although this is bound to happen occasionally, it is not uncommon for this to become a regularly occurring issue for some couples.

This term can also be used to describe a situation in which a couple is having multiple conversations per day about the betrayal. This situation usually happens when a wounded spouse is trying to "connect the dots" of information in order to wrap their head around how the betrayal happened. Agony, fear, and pressure are usually felt by the wounded spouse during this time. The person who has been unfaithful often feels a sense of dread and helplessness.

Other situations in which marathon conversations occur are:

1. When the wounded partner asks a question, and the wounding partner seems evasive or even outright refuses to answer.

2. The wounding partner tries to defend their behavior or blame shift

3. The wounded partner refuses to believe the answers they are given and decides to keep digging. This can possibly indicate that the wounded spouse has given relational meaning to certain infidelity-related behavior.

4. The wounded partner is verbally attacking the wounding partner out of pain and/or a need for punishment or revenge.

In all of the above-described scenarios, the wounded partner needs to understand the totality of the situation and is unlikely or unable to stop until they feel satisfied. Some of the reasons for this can include:

1. They want to get to the bottom of a particular issue

2. They are emotionally out of control and can't stop

3. They need to prove and point and/or be validated

4. They want to teach the wounding partner a lesson and/or use the information to get the wounding partner to "wake up" to what they have done

Wounding partners can get caught up in marathon conversations because:

1. They want to minimize or defend their behavior, so they don't feel so badly

2. They want the wounded partner to take at least part of the blame

3. They want the wounded partner to understand that they are actually wrong about something they are saying, thinking that "if they only understood, they would feel better"

4. They are triggered and/or angry

5. They are afraid to end the conversation for fear of being seen as uncaring or unwilling to try

It may seem counterintuitive, but the couples that are the most successful with navigating triggers and conversations around betrayal place time limits on their interactions around the subject. Short conversations (around 30-45 minutes in length) can be productive, while longer conversations are generally exhausting and typically get the couple nowhere. Also, the time you have your discussions will determine how productive they will be. We never recommend having discussions directly before bedtime.

At some point, conversations around the infidelity need to end because constantly digging up the past keeps the relationship from being able to move forward. However, this can vary depending on several different factors. If marathon conversations continue to be an issue for you, we highly recommend enlisted the help of a trained professional to assist you in getting past it.

Pitfall #4: Staying in denial

Although we don't see this as frequently as some of the other issues we have outlined here, we see it often enough that it warrants mentioning. We typically become concerned that this may be an issue for a couple when we hear reports of the following:

- One or both partners drops out of recovery early on

- Thinking the relationship is suddenly better because one or both partners knows more about recovery than they used to

- The couple is not talking about, or hardly ever talks about, the infidelity

- Infidelity-related behavior was discovered but there has been no real disclosure process or discussions since

- One or both partners seem overly distracted with work, activities, etc.

- The couple is engaging in "normal" behavior such as sex, vacations, family get togethers, etc. despite discovery or disclosure being new and reports that it is upsetting to the wounded partner

The truth is that betrayal in a relationship drastically changes things. While it doesn't have to mean that the relationship is doomed, it is important that both partners accept the fact that their reality has now changed. Couples and individuals struggling with denial are attempting to avoid the grief associated with the painful losses that betrayal represents. For wounded partners, these losses often include a loss of trust, safety, and a feeling of being able to depend on the wounding partner. For wounding partners, these losses can include the loss of the comfort associated with the infidelity-related behavior, the loss of positive self-image and a sense of honor, or a loss of the wounded partner's respect and admiration.

Although we understand that it may be tempting for one or both partners to remain in denial about the new situation that the discovery or disclosure of infidelity has created, here are some reasons why staying in denial isn't a good idea:

- It can cause one or both partners to ignore deeper personal issues that need to be dealt with.

- It can cause preexisting issues to be ignored.

- It can cause partners to become frustrated with themselves or the other person when any issues related to the betrayal arise.

- It can cause marathon fights because, once triggered, all of the issues come out at once.

- It can contribute to the wounding partner's relapse.

- It can set one or both partners up for physical and mental health issues due to the suppression of emotions.

- It can lead to distance between partners.

- It can deny both partners an opportunity for true intimacy.

Even though it can be tempting to pretend everything is "business as usual", each partner must be willing to deal with the challenges that betrayal presents if recovery is truly to take place. Although the idea of having tough conversations can be anxiety-producing, avoidance of those conversations will only serve to maintain that anxiety to the detriment of each partner and to the relationship overall.

Pitfall #5: Believing that the process should be quick

While we wish we could tell you that recovery from betrayal is a quick process, we can't. The truth is that recovery often takes couples an average of eighteen months to two years to achieve. In many cases, depending on the circumstances, it can take even longer. The rebuilding of trust is a long and time-consuming process. It is also an ongoing process that can be derailed if one or both partners fail to nurture it. This is not to say that a couple will not experience victories in communication and intimacy along the way. However, most couples report that it takes at least a solid eighteen months before they feel the relationship has begun to stabilize. Additionally, it is not uncommon for new realizations to hit the wounded partner years down the line and/or for anniversaries to continue to trigger intense emotions. Engaging in honest and safe communication around these issues and getting professional help when needed is the best way to move past this.

We don't write this to discourage you, but we want you to be prepared to have patience with yourself and with the process. There is simply no way to shortcut the rebuilding of trust after betrayal. There are, however, some ways that will prolong it or make it impossible. These are:

- Defending, blaming, or minimizing on the part of the wounding partner
- Explosive or inappropriate displays of anger on the part of the wounded partner
- Dribbling disclosure
- Continued mind-reading or unsubstantiated accusations on the part of the wounded partner
- Refusal to talk about the betrayal on the part of the wounding partner
- Marathon conversations that exhaust both partners
- Continued lying or engagement in infidelity-related behavior on the part of the wounding partner

Research shows that couples who can talk about infidelity in a constructive way on a regular basis tend to recover more quickly than those who don't. Therefore, it is imperative that the wounding partner engage in the recovery process and not shut the wounded partner down or refuse to answer questions. Although rebuilding trust is not a quick process, it can be done if both partners are committed to providing safety in the relationship.

PART 18

Recovery Plans

In order to help rebuild trust in a relationship after betrayal, recovery plans are essential when a couple is trying to reestablish safety. During our group and individual intensives, we work with couples to help them develop both relationship and individual recovery plans. These plans provide boundaries for both the wounding and wounded partner and can help keep the relationship on track. The plans that we discuss during intensives include:

- Communication Plan Ground Rules (Part I of the Communication Plan)
- Trigger Plan (Part II of the Communication Plan)
- Time-Out Protocol (Part III of the Communication Plan)
- Self-Care Plan
- Individual Recovery Plans

In the next few chapters, we will take a look at each of these in greater detail. First, let's look at the ground rules for the communication plan:

Recovery Plan #1: Communication plan (ground rules)

This is the first part of a three-part Communication Plan. Communication can be a challenge even for couples who aren't trying to recover from betrayal. However, when infidelity enters the mix, even the best communicators often have trouble. Although establishing safe communication can be difficult, it is worth the effort. Once both partners can express themselves and be understood, a deep sense of intimacy can be experienced, and the relationship can be strengthened.

If intimacy is to be restored, it is important that both partners agree on some ground rules for communication. This typically includes a system for both speaking and listening as well as a list of off-limit behaviors. We find that the Speaker-Listener technique is a simple and effective tool for couples who want to avoid conversations that spin out of control and go nowhere.

Speaker/Listener Technique

Each person takes turns speaking. You can have a "speaker object" if you are the speaker (such as a ball or a card), or just trade off.

Speaker Rules:

1. Use I statements only, such as "I felt sad when...."

2. Speak only for yourself (don't interject opinion, assumptions, or "mind reading")

3. Be respectful

4. Keep your statements brief and to the point (your partner can't paraphrase you if you go on and on)

5. Stop frequently to let the listener paraphrase

Listener Rules:

1. Paraphrase what you heard by saying, "what I heard you say is _____. Is that correct?"

2. If you weren't correct with what you paraphrased, the speaker should say "no" and say it again

3. Keep repeating this process until you get the paraphrasing correct.

4. Once the paraphrasing is correct, ask, "is there more?"

5. DO NOT rebut

6. DO NOT problem solve

7. When the speaker is done, validate what they said by saying something like, "It makes sense you could feel that way because…."

8. Show empathy for their experience

Rules for Both People:

1. The speaker always has the floor.

2. The speaker keeps the floor until they have said what they have to say.

3. Equal time should be given to each person to have the floor and to be heard.

4. Be respectful

5. After the speaker has said what they have to say and feels heard, the partners should switch roles.

6. WARNING: If the next speaker uses their turn to invalidate, rebut, or defend, all communication progress will be lost.

When using the Speaker-Listener technique, the object is to listen to, empathize with, and care about what the other person is saying.

In addition to using an effective system for speaking and listening, we also recommend that couples make a list of behaviors that they agree will be off-limits in terms of communication. Some of the more common of these include:

- Name-calling and insults
- Defending and blame-shifting
- Stonewalling
- Acting annoyed or inconvenienced
- Threatening
- Eye-rolling and other non-verbal signs of disrespect
- Character assassinations
- Always and never statements
- Predicting what the other person is going to say or do or saying things like, "I knew you would do that".

This is only a partial list of some of the most common mistakes couples make when trying to communicate. We recommend that couples make a list of specific things that pertain to them and agree ahead of time that these behaviors will be off limits.

Well-known author and psychotherapist Terrence Real outlines his five winning and losing strategies when it comes to communication in his book *The New Rules of Marriage*. According to Real, the five losing strategies are:

1. Right fighting. An argument about who is more right in the situation.

2. Controlling your partner. An argument where at least one partner is trying to control the other one. This is often done through aggression (yelling, threatening, blaming, etc.) or manipulation (guilting, shaming, twisting words, playing the victim, etc.)

3. Unbridled self-expression. An argument where at least one partner says whatever they are thinking in the heat of the moment to the other partner with no filter of kindness, compassion, or respect.

4. Retaliation. An argument where at least one partner says something to purposely hurt the other one as a way of paying the person back for hurting them in some way. This can be overt or passive aggressive.

5. Withdrawal. An argument that leads to one or both partners withdrawing out of frustration, resignation, or retaliation (silent treatment). Not to be confused with taking a proper time out.0

Terrence Real's five winning strategies are:

1. Shift from complaint to request. It is often easier to complain about someone than to make requests for what we need. Requesting requires vulnerability while complaining puts the speaker in a one-up position. Switch from complaints to requests and make your requests behavioral and reasonable.

2. Speak to repair with love and respect. Commit, along with your partner, to the repair process. Remember love when speaking.

3. Respond with generosity. Listen to understand (this doesn't mean you have to agree). Clarify to make sure you understand what your partner is saying. Acknowledge whatever you can without rebuttal. Give whatever you can to your partner.

4. Empower each other. Acknowledge any gifts your partner has brought to the conversation. Ask how you can help your partner. Give whatever you can.

5. Cherish each other. Give your partner feedback and positive affirmations daily. Practice generosity. Nourish the relationship with your time and energy.

Recovery Plan #2: Trigger plan

The Trigger Plan is the second part of the three-part Communication Plan. Communicating when someone has been triggered requires not only great communication skills, but some forethought as well. Triggers and reminders are a normal part of the recovery process. A frustrating and painful part of recovery-but a normal part, nonetheless. They are simply a part of dealing with trauma. Studies have shown that partners dealing with betrayal trauma are coping with a great number of triggers per day in the weeks and months following disclosure. We have had wounded partners tell us that, especially early on in recovery, they deal with 75+ triggers per day. If the wounding partner's disclosure was "dribbled" out over time, each instance of new information causes a separate trauma for the wounded partner, which makes dealing with triggers much more complex. This is why we recommend being 100% upfront and honest during the disclosure process.

Triggers, reminders, flashbacks, and the like kick the wounded partner's sympathetic nervous system into high gear. This part of the system is responsible for survival. When triggered, the body undergoes multiple changes in preparation for a physical response to threat. These include:

- Increased breathing rate
- Increased heart rate
- Muscle tension
- Changes to facial coloring (increased redness or paleness)
- Sweating
- Shaking, especially of the hands
- Rise in body temperature

These changes take place because the autonomic nervous system (which the sympathetic nervous system is a part of) floods the body with stress hormones such as adrenaline and cortisol. Additionally, blood flow is redirected from the gut to the muscles, and especially the hands, in preparation for physical exertion in the form of fighting. The arousal caused by all of this is very intense and can take from several hours to a few days to fully recover from. During this slow cool-down period, a person has a higher-than-normal likelihood of being retriggered and/or responding intensely to even minor triggers. One can see how this could create a problem for the wounded partner who has been traumatized and is getting re-triggered frequently throughout the day. Due to these constant triggers and reminders, a betrayed partner can be thrown into a vicious cycle of anger. This is one of the main explanations of why wounded partners can get, and stay, so angry. Depending on the personality of the triggered person, they may go on the attack, physically leave, or emotionally check out.

It is important that the wounding partner understand that, when the wounded partner becomes triggered and floods with emotion, that it is not an attempt on their part to punish them or make them suffer. It is simply a normal bodily reaction to the presence of a threat—real or perceived. Triggers are also not a sign that the wounded partner does not forgive the wounding partner. This is especially important for people who hold to religions where forgiveness is fundamental. We get wounded partners in our office on a regular basis that have been told by well-meaning counselors and/or by their partners that they are being unforgiving and need to work on it. This is simply not the case. As we stated previously, triggers are a normal part of the recovery process when it comes to infidelity. The wounded partner does not have control over where and when triggers come up. Triggers and reminders are a normal consequence of the primary bond that has been severed between the wounding and wounded partners because of betrayal.

Many couples we work with think that, when triggers show up, they are having a setback. This is not true either. Instead, we would like to present the idea that the triggers present opportunities for repair and intimacy between partners. If the wounding partner will show up with love and empathy when the wounded partner is triggered, it presents a unique opportunity for the wounding partner to change how the wounded partner sees them and, therefore, help increase connection. Additionally, if the wounded partner will openly talk about their pain and emotions without name-calling, threatening, etc., the relationship can grow in intimacy.

For the wounded partner, it is important to start managing their triggers in a productive way early on. We recommend that a trigger journal be kept by the wounded partner that identifies the following about each trigger:

1. What was the trigger?

2. What was I doing when it happened?

3. Was the wounding partner present? If so, what were they doing?

4. What time of day did the trigger happen?

5. Why do I think it happened?

Once a trigger has been identified, the wounded partner can answer the following questions about it:

1. Is what I am reacting to a current situation? (examples: wounding partner is defending, wounding partner is hiding their phone, etc.)

2. Is what I am reacting to a past situation? (example: a memory or a reminder)

3. Am I reacting to holes in the wounding partner's story? (example: wounding partner gave an account of events, but something doesn't make sense)

4. Am I reacting to a loss of connection with my partner? (example: the wounding partner withdrew, and it felt like abandonment)

As the wounded partner keeps a journal, they might begin to see patterns emerging. If a pattern is identified, they can dig deeper in order to identify specifically what trigger is associated with what pattern. For example, the wounded partner may notice that they are triggered in a certain type of place. This knowledge will then help them investigate further to find out what the trigger is really about. Although many triggers are obvious and can be added to the "Identifying Triggers" exercise below right away, some triggers may be harder to identify. Keeping a trigger journal can help the wounded partner do that.

Having conversations around how to deal with triggers can be hard for many couples, but it is imperative that these conversations happen if the couple hopes to successfully work through them. Oftentimes, the wounding partner wants to do something to help the wounded partner but doesn't know where to begin, and the wounded partner feels just as helpless. A trigger plan is extremely helpful for both partners to know what to do when a trigger arises. At a calm time, establish a plan for when triggers come. It is important not to do this in the heat of the moment. This can be somewhat counter-intuitive because, when things are going well, the subject of infidelity is not typically what either partner wants to be talking about. However, this exercise requires rational thought, which is impossible when the sympathetic nervous system is triggering either partner into "fight, flight, or freeze" mode.

While making the plan, the wounding partner should ask the wounded partner questions like:

1. What would help you feel safe when you are triggered?

2. What can I do?

3. Can you help me understand what's going on with you?

4. What do I do that makes you feel unsafe during these times?

The answers to these and other questions will help develop your plan. Please note that the plan should be considered an official agreement between the wounded and wounding partners. It must be adhered to in order to work. Wounding partners: **going off script, defending, walling off, or leaving will only serve to escalate the situation and re-wound your partner.** Wounded partners: **threatening, shaming, yelling, and name-calling will short-circuit the process.** When developing a trigger plan, start with the "Identifying Triggers" exercise below.

Identifying Triggers

Specific Triggers	How does this apply to your situation?	Action plan
Seeing attractive people (with or without partner)		Hold your partner's hand if in public
Sex scenes in movies + TV		Change the channel Research programs before watching
Inconsistency/ unreliability of partner (e.g., being late)		Express concerns to partner gently
Times of day Days of the week (e.g., weekends, late nights)		Plan ahead to do something relaxing

Other:		
Other:		
Other:		

Notice that the "Identifying Triggers" table has a column entitled "Action Plan". Each trigger needs an action plan attached to it. This should be something that the wounded partner feels that the wounding partner can do to help the situation.

Next, fill out the "Trigger Coping Plan for Couples":

Trigger Coping Plan for Couples

The main triggers in our relationship are:	

Strategies for managing triggers:	
Time-out / alone time	
Making a request (e.g., for a hug, reassurance)	
Talking about it (using "I" statements)	
Behaviors to avoid:	

These tools have proven to be extremely effective for couples who are dealing with triggers. However, we acknowledge that there are times when an unexpected trigger arises that there was no plan for. In this case, the couple should adhere to the agreements made in the Communication Plan plus use the following guidelines:

1. Wounded Partner: Recognize the trigger and accept that it is happening.

2. Wounding Partner: If you notice that your partner is triggered and flooded with emotion, do not point it out to them. This never helps. Instead, ask them what they need from you in this moment. If they don't know, just let them know you are there for them.

3. Wounded Partner: Identify what you are reacting to. Is it something that is currently happening? Is it a reminder from the past? Is it a loss of connection with your partner?

4. Wounding Partner: Identify if you are also being triggered. If so, by what? Is it guilt and/or shame? Is it your partner's emotions?

5. Wounded Partner: Identify at least one thing that your partner can do in this moment to help you.

6. Wounding Partner: If possible, do whatever your partner is asking of you. Respond with humility, patience, and compassion.

7. Wounding Partner: Resist talking about how bad you feel and/or saying, "I'm sorry" immediately. Instead, use the Speaker/Listener technique from the Communication Plan to ensure that your partner feels heard.

8. Wounded and Wounding Partners: Avoid any of the "off-limits" behaviors outlined in your communication plan.

Recovery Plan #3: Time Out Protocol

The Time Out Protocol is the final piece of the three-part Communication Plan. There will likely be occasions when one or both partners become overwhelmed with emotions to the point that they can't function in a way that will support the health of the relationship. When someone is flooded with emotion, they may say or do things that attack the other person—adding even more pain to an already painful situation.

As a countermeasure to overwhelming emotions, the couple should develop a code word or a non-verbal sign that is an indicator that one of them needs to stop talking before they do more damage than good. Once a code word is spoken or a non-verbal sign is shown, the couple will disengage and agree to come back later when things have calmed down. The couple should agree to the terms of time out ahead of time and consider the Time Out Plan to be a contract between the two parties like the other parts of the Communication Plan.

There are five main points to keep in mind when considering whether or not to call a time out:

1. USE THE CODE WORD or NON-VERBAL SIGN SPARINGLY. Time outs are considered an emergency option when all attempts at productive communication have failed. Understand that if either partner uses their code word or non-verbal sign to get out of conversations that they just don't want to deal with, they are hurting their partner. Using the code word or non-verbal sign to stonewall is also an improper use of a time out.

2. The request for time out should be honored. One partner should not try to goad the other into reengaging. The conversation needs to stop when time out is called. No attempting to have the last word.

3. When a code word or non-verbal sign has been used, agree on a time to reengage. Otherwise, one or both partners could feel neglected and abandoned. Typically, 20-30 minutes is recommended for a time out.

4. When a time out is taken, it is recommended that each person practice self-care. This means that an activity should be done to take the mind OFF the present problem, as opposed to taking the time to stew about it and/or plan a rebuttal. Reading a book (not on the subject of the argument or betrayal), taking a shower/bath, or taking a walk are great activities to do. Time-outs do not work if either party uses the time to sit around and think about how angry they are or what they are going to say next in an effort to win the argument. The idea is to take your mind completely off the

argument in order to give your flooded system a break.

5. When you come back from the time out, each partner needs to state at least one thing they appreciate about the other before resuming the conversation. When sharing feelings, use "I feel" statements as opposed to "you" statements. "You" statements come off as blaming. Blaming and/or criticizing will only make the problem worse. Focus on the solution as opposed to the problem(s) and be good listeners.

As with the Trigger Plan, the Time Out Plan should be developed at a calm moment.

PART 19

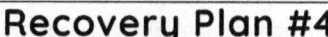

Recovery Plan #4

Self-Care Plan

The term "self-care" encompasses the idea that human beings need to take care of themselves so that they can accomplish the tasks that they need to get done. Self-care is part of the answer to how we can effectively deal with stressors in our lives. When dealing with the aftermath of betrayal, both partners face a wide range of stressors that can seriously impede on the ability to maintain their health, do well at their jobs, maintain friendships, and care for their children or other people who depend on them.

Self-care means taking care of yourself in every area, not just physically. Good self-care includes the physical, spiritual, emotional/mental, social, and financial aspects of life. It also involves engaging in active recovery. Let's take a look at each one of the areas of self-care more closely:

Physical: This includes anything pertaining to our bodies. Examples of physical self-care include healthy eating, exercise, drinking plenty of water, good sleep hygiene, and even leisurely activities such as taking a bath or getting a massage. It can also include regularly going to the doctor for health checkups.

Spiritual: It is important to take care of our spiritual side. Self-care in this area can include meditation, prayer, going to church, practicing mindfulness, connecting with God through nature, and reading spiritual literature.

Emotional/Mental: Our emotional and mental health is vital to our well-being. Self-care in this area could include listening to music, engaging in coaching or counseling, reading a good book, listening to helpful podcasts, and making a gratitude list (this one could also be counted as spiritual).

Social: It is important that partners don't isolate themselves when dealing with the challenges presented by betrayal. Self-care in this area could include scheduling regular phone calls with supportive friends and family, texting with friends and family, joining a support group and reaching out to other members, spending time with people you care about, attending social events, and going out on dates with your partner in order to provide time for much-needed reconnection.

Financial: A number of our clients claim they feel at a disadvantage because they have chosen to stay at home. For many, this creates an imbalance of power within the relationship which has an even greater impact after infidelity is discovered or disclosed. While staying at home and caring for the household is an extremely important job that doesn't get as much respect as it deserves, partners who stay at home often describe feelings of disempowerment and "stuckness" when it comes to their choice of whether or not to stay in the relationship because they are completely financially dependent on their partner. If this describes you, some ideas for self-care in this area could include gaining job skills, becoming more involved in the financial aspect of the relationship, or going back to work. Even if you don't feel stuck or disempowered in this area, going back to school, getting a job, or starting a new business can give you an added boost for your self-esteem.

Another financial area that often gets affected by betrayal is when the wounding partner spends money that belongs to both partners on their infidelity-related behavior. In this example, self-care could include ongoing accountability and transparency with finances moving forward.

Engaging in Active Recovery: When it comes to the damage done by betrayal, it is vitally important that both partners take charge of their own recovery. Reading this book is a sign that you are doing that already. Other ideas could include counseling or coaching, workgroups, reading self-help literature, and attending Becoming Well intensives, seminars, and conferences designed to support your healing.

Self-care is all about engaging in activities that benefit you. An important thing to realize about self-care is that it is not always about relaxing. In fact, it will often require you to expend energy on healthy activities or engage mentally with things that might feel uncomfortable. The purpose of self-care is to heal underlying issues and refuel so that you can deal with the challenges presented by betrayal. As important as it is to identify areas and ways that partners can take care of themselves, it is equally important to identify things that can detract from recovery. Here are some things that self-care is not:

- Being so busy with tasks or helping others that you become depleted
- Overindulging in food or spending
- Using addictive substances such as drugs and alcohol to cope with unwanted and/or unpleasant feelings
- Failing to control what you do and say in anger
- Neglecting your responsibilities

Although many of the activities listed here can seem appealing, they will not do anything to refuel you, and some can leave you stressed with feelings of guilt and shame.

Self-care is never as important as when a relationship is facing the aftermath of infidelity. The burden of the tsunami of intense feelings and emotional distress that accompany recovery can leave partners feeling seriously depleted. The danger for partners is expending all of their energy to fix the crisis the relationship is facing. For wounded partners in particular, the hypervigilance born out of betrayal can become all-consuming. It is important that a wounded partner take a step back, breathe, and understand that they can't immediately fix everything- as much as they might like to do so. Taking time to focus on self-care isn't selfish and will end up helping the relationship in the long run.

In our experience, there are several ways that partners engage in activities in the name of self-care that are actually self-care sabotage. The most common of these are:

- An overindulgence in self-soothing

- Unrestrained gratification of desires (self-indulgence)

- Laziness

Although these things are okay once in a while, an overindulgence in any of them typically sabotages recovery. The hard part is that self-care sabotage can actually feel like self-care in the moment. Self-care only works if a person uses it to grow- not if they use it to let themselves off the hook or avoid accountability. Here are some helpful questions that you can ask yourself in order to figure out if you are engaging in self-care or self-care sabotage:

- Will this activity support my overall well-being or the well-being of my relationship?

- Am I willing to let this challenge me, or am I avoiding being challenged?

- Am I isolating myself, or am I just resting up?
- Am I taking an active role in my recovery?
- Am I trying to escape or avoid something by choosing this activity?
- Does this activity connect me to myself and/or others, or do I feel disconnected?
- Am I going to feel better or worse after doing this activity?
- Am I indulging anger or self-pity by doing this activity?
- Will I be able to do the things I need to do better after doing this activity?

Another way that partners can sabotage self-care is by simply not setting aside time for it. Waiting for the schedule to "open up" so that you can care for yourself is not the best plan of action. Interruptions, unplanned events, distractions, and emotional and physical exhaustion can cause partners to constantly come in last when it comes to caring for themselves. If a person wants to succeed with self-care, it needs to be prioritized. Here are some ways you can make caring for yourself a priority:

- Set aside specific times and days for self-care activities
- Wake up a bit earlier
- Break up self-care time into small chunks
- Choose activities that you enjoy, especially when it comes to physical exercise
- Find an accountability partner
- Hire a babysitter if you have children
- Reduce time spent on social media, tv, or streaming services

- Use an alarm as a reminder
- Set specific goals
- Eliminate hurdles to self-care
- Communicate your goals to others
- Plan adequate time for activities (don't be a "time optimist")
- Create boundaries around self-care and be assertive with them
- Engage in short self-care activities often

Each partner should take the time to fill out the Self-Care Worksheet and the Self-Care Worksheet Schedule for themselves. At a calm time, you should discuss your individual plans with each other so that you can be on the same page and can support each other in your self-care efforts.

Self-Care Worksheet

Activities that support my physical well-being

Answer:	

Activities that support my spiritual well-being

Answer:	

Activities that support my emotional/mental well-being

Answer:	

Activities that support my social well-being

Answer:	

Activities that support my financial well-being

Answer:	

Activities that support my active recovery

Answer:	

Self-Care Worksheet Schedule

Activity	Day	Time

PART 20

Recovery Plan #5

Individual Recovery Plans

Individual recovery plans for both the wounded and wounding partners are just that—individual. As such, it would take us pages upon pages to list all of the possibilities that might go into a person's recovery plan. Instead, we would like to highlight some of the areas commonly addressed. First, we will cover what typically goes into the wounding partner's recovery plan.

For the wounding partner, a recovery plan typically includes a relapse prevention plan as well. Here are the topics most commonly addressed:

- Pornography and/or sexually stimulating images
- Grooming behaviors
- Accountability phone calls
- Groups
- Coaching or counselling
- Recovery material such as books and workbooks
- Intimacy avoidant behavior
- Sexually anorexic behavior

- Accountability partners
- Gratitude
- Connection exercises with partner such as daily affirmations and weekly dates
- Entitlement
- Defensiveness, blame, playing the victim
- Lying
- Self-care
- Relapse research
- Replacements
- 24-hour tell policy
- Polygraph schedule
- Pornography blockers
- Location trackers
- Sex establishments
- Media boundaries (computer, phone, etc.)
- Contact with affair partner

As you can see, the list of things included in a wounding partner's recovery and relapse prevention plan is long. This is because we see clients with intimacy avoidance, sexual and emotional infidelity, and infidelity through pornography. Due to the wide range of issues, there are a number of things that have to be addressed depending on the specific issues with each individual. While most of these items don't need much explanation in terms of why being accountable for them is applicable to ongoing recovery, we would like to go more in-depth into the subjects of grooming behaviors, intimacy avoidant behavior, sexually anorexic behavior, gratitude, relapse research, replacements, and contact with an affair partner.

Grooming behavior: Grooming is a form of manipulation in which the person doing the grooming builds an emotional connection or rapport with another person that appears to be genuine. The motives underlying grooming behavior can be numerous, but typically involve control and/or sex. Grooming is marked by the groomer's desire to have a particular need met, despite what it may cost themselves, their partner, or the other person.

Grooming behavior is most associated with people who have a sexual addiction. We most often see this type of behavior in wounding partners who have engaged in multiple affairs and one-night stands. It is important to note that not all sexual addicts groom. However, when they do, it typically includes flirting, touching and/or hugging, revealing personal details about themselves, rescuing someone out of their circumstances, offering emotional support and/or encouragement, and complimenting.

Intimacy avoidant behavior: The term intimacy avoidance refers to a situation in which one partner is withholding themselves in multiple ways from the other partner. Intimacy avoidance often goes unnoticed by the person withholding themselves yet can have lasting and devastating effects on their loved ones. Intimacy anorexic behaviors are intentional and include the withholding of emotional, physical, sexual, and/or spiritual connection from a partner for the purpose of creating distance and/or maintaining power and control. The difference between the two is intent.

Intimacy avoidant and intimacy anorexic behaviors can include ongoing criticism of the partner (often unwarranted), playing the victim when called on bad behavior, refraining from showing love in the way their partner wants to be loved, being too busy to spend time with the partner and/or being emotionally unavailable, offering little to no praise to their partner, and an unwillingness or inability to express emotions—especially to partner.

Sexually anorexic behavior: Sexual anorexia is a condition marked by the fear, dread, or avoidance of sexual activity. Although it can be marked by impotence or other physical problems, the cause is typically psychological.

Although we have seen some sexual anorexics who avoid sex in any setting, sexual anorexia is most commonly seen in connection to the anorexic's partner. This is because the root of the problem is typically a fear of intimacy. We often see sexual anorexia in conjunction with sexual and/or pornography addiction, intimacy avoidance, and intimacy anorexia. It is not uncommon for sexual anorexics to engage in sex outside of their primary relationship yet withhold sex from their primary partner. It is also extremely common for sexual anorexics to engage in pornography and masturbation.

If the wounding partner displays signs of sexual anorexia, a sexual schedule is typically included in the individual recovery plan—provided that the wounded partner feels ready to engage in sex.

Gratitude: Many of the clients we work with engage in negative thinking about their partner and/or their life in general. Keeping a running gratitude list is one of the ways to help combat this.

Relapse research: Relapse is unfortunate, but it does happen sometimes in early recovery. When our clients relapse, we want them to take stock of what happened and work with us and their accountability partners to try to figure out how it can be avoided in the future. The following relapse research questions were adapted from the book *101 Freedom Exercises* by Douglas Weiss, Ph.D.:

- What were my feelings prior to acting out?
- What red flags did I pass up?
- What recovery tools did I choose not to use?
- How many days have I been thinking about/planning this event?
- What was the cost associated with my acting out?
- What did I learn about myself from this relapse?
- What do I need to do differently?
- Do I need to change any boundaries to avoid this in the future?
- Who am I going to share this information with to help me stay accountable?

Replacements: It is important to note that the wounding partner should look to replace undesired and/or unacceptable behaviors with new, productive ones. An example of this would be replacing pornography and masturbation with stress-relieving exercise such as running or biking. These activities can boost mood, train the body on how to deal with anxiety, and lead to a sense of accomplishment that can boost well-being. (Weir, 2011) It is important to replace unwanted habits, especially in the case of addiction, with healthy ones. Otherwise, a person is likely to be pulled back toward the undesirable behavior because of the rewards associated with it.

For the wounded partner, an individual recovery plan could include the following:

- Trigger journal (covered previously)
- Off-limits behavior list
- Replacements
- Accountability
- Support group
- Self-care
- Classes
- Recovery material such as books or workbooks
- Coaching or counseling
- Safe friends

Many of these items don't need much explanation in terms of why they would be included in the wounded partner's plan for ongoing recovery. However, we would like to go more in-depth into the subjects of the off-limits behaviors list, replacements, accountability, and classes.

Off-limits behaviors list: We want to preface this by stating that we are in no way implying that the wounded partner should take any of the blame for the wounding partner's behavior. However, as we mentioned previously, there are some behaviors that wounded partners engage in once betrayal has been discovered or disclosed that are not conducive to the recovery of the relationship. Behaviors such as yelling, threatening, name-calling, and/or shaming on an ongoing basis will tear at the fabric of an already-fragile relationship to the point that safety cannot be established. These types of behaviors are what should be included on the off-limits behaviors list and the wounded partner should work diligently in overcoming the need to engage in them.

Replacements: The wounded partner should replace undesirable behaviors with new, desirable ones. Acting out in anger can have its own addictive quality to it because it involves adrenaline and often feels empowering. If the wounded partner does not find healthy ways to nurture themselves when they are hurt and angry, chances are that they might fall back into engaging in angry outbursts.

Accountability: It is important that wounded partners do not attempt to do recovery alone. There are several areas where accountability could be necessary for a wounded partner. Some of the most common include acting out in anger, isolating, and not enforcing boundaries with the wounding partner.

Classes: At Becoming Well, we offer classes specifically designed for wounded partners who want to heal after the disclosure or discovery of betrayal. Visit our website at **www.mybecomingwell.com** to learn more.

PART 21

Recovery Plan #6

Plan for cutting off contact with an affair partner

As we stated previously, the wounding partner's failure to end infidelity-related behavior is the number one reason we see relationships fail to recover after infidelity has been discovered or disclosed. This is especially true for couples dealing with betrayal through emotional and/or sexual affairs. When the wounding partner fails to cut off contact with an affair partner it creates a lack of safety for the wounded partner which will interfere with recovery.

If you are a wounded partner reading this and your partner has not completely cut off contact with their affair partner, it is important that you put a boundary in place to keep yourself safe. It is also important that you understand that the wounding partner cannot be forced into making the decision to cut ties with an affair partner. As painful as it can be for you to wait for the wounding partner to act, cutting off contact takes a willingness and a commitment on their part that cannot be forced. This is especially true in the case of limerent affairs because the pull is so strong that much effort is required to maintain distance from the affair partner.

Does this mean that you simply have to put up with your partner's behavior? Certainly not. However, it is more effective for you as a wounded partner to distance themselves from your partner and give them a time limit to end the affair than it is to plead with or threaten them. We understand that this information might be extremely upsetting to you. While we certainly understand why it would be, we feel obligated to tell you that we have seen many cases where pleading and threatening on the wounded partner's part actually pushes the wounding partner closer to their affair partner. Additionally, we would advise that you not offer more sex to your partner in hopes of luring them back. In our experience, this leads the wounding partner to indulge in a situation where they can have their cake and eat it too. When the wounding partner engages in infidelity-related behavior and the wounded partner gives them more sex, they are actually rewarding the bad behavior. As a result, the wounding partner has little incentive to change their ways.

If you are a wounding partner reading this and are still in contact with an affair partner, we urge you to adopt a no-contact rule. Your relationship will not be able to recover in any meaningful way until you do this because you are creating an unsafe situation for your partner. This is going to require a sincere commitment on your part. We recommend that you take the following steps to end the contact:

- You need to firmly decide that you are going to end things for the good of your relationship. This is different from wishing that you could end things. If you do not make a firm decision to end contact, you are likely to be pulled back at some point.

- Write a letter to remind yourself why you are choosing to end contact with the affair partner. Read it often.

- Take responsibility for ending the contact and firmly state that you are the one deciding to end things. Do not put it off onto the wounded partner to end things for you.

- Don't say things to your affair partner like, "I'll always miss you, but I have to do this" or, "I wish I could still be with you, but…". This leaves ambiguity in the situation. Instead, firmly state that you are ending contact and leave it there.

- Don't tell your affair partner that you can still be friends. This leaves too much wiggle room for you to contact them and/or them to contact you. Over means over.

- Remember that the affair partner might get upset, but your loyalty belongs to your partner—not to them.

- Decide ahead of time what you will do if they reach out to you. State this clearly when you are ending things.

- Do not cut off contact by engaging in a face-to-face meeting with the affair partner. Email or phone call will suffice.

- Clearly state to the affair partner that this decision is what you want.

- Involve the wounded partner in drafting the email to the affair partner. If you call them, make sure your partner is there with you.

- If the affair partner contacts you, do not answer. It may be wise for you to change your phone number and/or email address. Additionally, you will need to block them on all social media.

Once you have ended things, it is important that you understand your vulnerability and put guardrails in place in the form of accountability immediately. Although not an excuse, relapse is a part of change. Be aware of this and be vigilant to protect your relationship and your boundaries.

We advise that the wounding partner find motivation for ending contact with an affair partner outside of wanting to save the relationship. When it comes to recovery from betrayal, wishing to save the relationship is not a strong enough reason. As we stated previously, the process takes most couples approximately two years, during which time there will be many obstacles and much turmoil. Because the process is not easy or quick, it is common for one or both partners to want to throw in the towel at some point. This is why the motivation for following through with the commitment to each other needs to come from a deeper place. For some, this is a commitment to God. For others, it is a commitment to integrity and/or morals. Whatever the personal motivation, the wounding partner should place a reminder for themselves somewhere that they can read often.

When it comes to holding to the commitment of no-contact, accountability is key. Ensuring that the wounding partner has people around them that will tell them the truth is of vital importance. This is why we include groups and accountability partners in the individual recovery plan. We have worked with many wounding partners who have the best of intentions but, at one point or another, fall into the trap of self-deception when it comes to what they can and can't manage. Putting people in place who will speak the truth will help the wounding partner gain clarity and perspective that can keep them from making decisions that will damage their partner. Additionally, it is important that the wounding partner engage with accountability and recovery partners because it provides a safe space for them to work out thoughts and feelings that might otherwise drag them toward making poor choices.

PART 22

Rebuilding Trust Pyramid Layer #3

Consistency

When betrayal is discovered or disclosed, it creates an enormous amount of uncertainty for the wounded partner. For them, the past, present, and future of the relationship are often all called into question. We work with many wounded partners that tell us they don't feel like they know their partner anymore and are suddenly experiencing doubt as to whether or not they ever really knew them at all. The trauma they experience from this break in attachment is intense and difficult to overcome. This is why consistency on the wounding partner's part is crucial to the rebuilding trust process. When the wounded partner sees consistency in the wounding partner, it builds trust because it begins to remove some of their uncertainty. Consistency will begin to show the wounded partner that the wounding partner is clear on what they want and are taking steps to reach their goals. It shows that they are committed to the relationship and understand the gravity of what they have done.

In the definitions section of this book we defined trust as "the ability to feel that one's partner is a source of security, support, safety, and dependability". We believe that the words "security", "support", "safety", and "dependability" are all related to the idea of consistency. What a person chooses to do consistently is a reflection of their true values and standards. This can show up as character strengths or character defects. For example, if a person consistently gaslights, minimizes, or defends, they are telling their partner that they value their own need to be right over that person's well-being. If a person consistently follows through on commitments, apologizes when wrong, and seeks to truly listen to what the other person is saying, it shows that they value that person and the relationship.

We read an article in *Forbes* a while back which outlined five areas as being associated with consistent, predictable, and reliable people. The author referred to these areas as "The Consistency Index" and, while he was referring to behavior in a professional environment, we feel that they apply to relationships in which infidelity has been an issue. The five areas are:

- Being a role model/setting a good example
- Avoiding saying one thing and doing another
- Honoring commitments and keeping promises
- Following through on commitments
- Showing a willingness to go above and beyond when necessary (Folkman, 2019)

As you move forward in your recovery, keeping these five areas in mind while evaluating your progress will go a long way in creating the consistency you need in order to rebuild trust

Consistency in behavior can lead the wounded partner to start to believe that the wounding partner is dependable, and this can eventually lead to trust.

Consistent and reliable behavior on the part of the wounding partner is comforting to the wounded partner because reliability is an indication that the wounding partner is focused on the relationship instead of solely on themselves.

This is crucial because self-focused behavior was what led to the infidelity-related behavior in the first place. If the wounded partner sees a continuation of this type of behavior, they will be unlikely to extend trust any time soon, if ever, to the wounding partner. Words will do little to soothe the pain of a wounded partner; consistent action over time is what is needed for trust to be rebuilt.

We feel a need to mention that it is not only important that the wounding partner show consistency in recovery, but it is important for the wounded partner to show consistency in their own recovery as well. As we have stated numerous times throughout this book, we are not implying that the wounded partner should take on any of the blame for the wounding partner's decision to engage in infidelity-related behavior. However, if the wounded partner consistently engages in angry outbursts, stonewalling or withdrawal, shaming, and threatening it will eventually end up damaging the relationship in a completely new and unfortunate way. We have worked with numerous couples that have come to us after years of trying to heal from betrayal on their own and are struggling to stay together. Aside from the wounding partner's infidelity-related behavior, we often see evidence that the wounded partner's behavior has made the rebuilding trust process far more difficult than it would have otherwise been. It is essential that **both** partners consistently adhere to communication ground rules, trigger plans, and time out protocols if the relationship is to recover.

While there are a few points in this chapter that address consistency on the part of the couple and/or the wounded partner, the majority of it will be dedicated to the wounding partner. Their consistency in individual recovery as well as in their focus on the relationship instead of on themselves is what will make the most difference—especially in the beginning phases of rebuilding trust. However, the lack of focus on the wounded partner does not imply that their own consistency in areas that they are responsible for is somehow less important.

Wounding Partner Consistency

Item #1: Keep the door shut (no-contact)

This one is specifically for wounding partners who have had sexual and/or emotional affairs. Although we highlighted steps that can be taken to go no-contact with an affair partner, we want to stress the importance of keeping the door shut to them. Trust during the recovery process is hard-earned, and nothing will break it down faster than if the wounding partner has contact with an affair partner. Even if the contact is mildly friendly with no sexual overtones, the wounded partner is likely to see any contact with an affair partner as another betrayal.

Although we previously covered accountability as a key component of holding fast to the no-contact rule, we also want to emphasize that it is important that the wounding partner have an overall plan in place. This plan should include several "how am I going to handle it…" scenarios. Some examples are:

- How am I going to handle it if my affair partner emails me?

- How am I going to handle it if my affair partner shows up at my work?

- How am I going to handle it if I am mad at my partner and miss my affair partner?

- How am I going to handle it if I start to romanticize the relationship with my affair partner again?

- How am I going to handle it if my affair partner texts or calls me from someone else's phone?

The list of possible scenarios is long, but hopefully you get the idea. It is important the wounding partner decide how they are going to handle these types of scenarios ahead of time. We advise that this plan is put into writing and that the wounding partner share it with the wounded partner along with at least one accountability partner. This plan is especially important for the wounding partner to develop immediately after betrayal because this is likely when they feel the most regretful about what has happened. If you are a wounding partner reading this, developing this plan early on and sharing it with people who can keep you accountable will help you stick to it when you are experiencing the prolonged turmoil that follows betrayal.

If the infidelity was pornography-related, we suggest that the wounding partner put monitoring software on all devices. Additionally, planning ahead is a must. Much like the "how am I going to handle it" scenarios listed above for stopping contact with an affair partner, the wounding partner with a pornography issue should make a list of possible scenarios where they might be tempted to look at pornography and make a plan for what they will do should that situation arise. These scenarios should not only include physical situations, but times when the wounding partner is likely to feel angry, lonely, tired, afraid, or any number of intense feelings that will tempt them to self-soothe with pornography and masturbation.

Item #2: Polygraph schedule

As described in the previous section on trust-building behaviors, the polygraph is a powerful instrument that can help pave the way to rebuilding trust in a relationship. It can provide a couple with a baseline of truth when there has been deception involved. Unfortunately, the word of the wounding partner often isn't enough for the wounded partner to feel safe and trusting. Due to the lies and deception typically involved, the wounding partner's assurances often mean little to nothing to the wounded partner. Consistent action is what they need to see. We often work with wounding partners who are frustrated with the fact that the wounded partner won't believe them when they say that they are sorry and promise to never do it again. If you are a wounding partner and this describes your situation, we would remind you that you likely made promises prior to your betrayal that you didn't uphold. It is unreasonable for you to expect that your words should be enough to fix things now.

For many couples, especially when sexual or pornography addiction is an issue, ongoing polygraphs are often an important component of rebuilding trust. A willingness on the wounding partner's part to take ongoing polygraphs can be an excellent way for them to show that they are being consistent with their recovery and have nothing to hide. When the wounding partner passes multiple polygraphs over a period of time, this aids in the wounded partner's feelings of overall safety in the relationship. If you are a wounding partner and are balking at the idea of taking multiple polygraphs, we would encourage you to see it as a gift you can give your partner that will help them. Additionally, especially if addiction to sex or pornography is an issue for you, it is a gift that you can give yourself because the ongoing accountability polygraphs provide will aid you in your recovery.

For those of you who wish to include a polygraph schedule as a component of the rebuilding trust process, we recommend that the wounding partner take a polygraph examination every 3-6 months for the first year, every 6 months for the second year, and once per year thereafter.

Item #3: Weekly check-ins

For wounding partners dealing with addiction and/or intimacy avoidance, activities such as meetings, accountability phone calls, workbooks, etc. are an integral part of the individual recovery plan. When we work with couples, we often hear from the wounded partner that they feel left out of this portion the recovery process. While the following check-in sheet is what we use for members of our group meetings, the sheet can also be used to report out to the wounded partner and keep them up to date on the wounding partner's progress:

I'm recovering from _____ (Sexual Addiction; Intimacy Anorexia, Emotional/Sexual Infidelity, being the Partner of an IA)

I'm also recovering from_____ trauma that I experienced when I was _____ by _____.

My SA Sobriety date is _____; I'm _____% responsible for the devastation and _____% responsible for my recovery from it

(No masturbation, touching self to arousal, intentionally viewing images for sexual arousal, fantasizing, for arousal during being sexual with spouse)

My Infidelity Sobriety date is _____; I'm _____% responsible for the devastation and _____% responsible for my recovery from it.

My IA Sobriety date is _____; I'm _____% responsible for the devastation and _____% responsible for my recovery from it.

(Sobriety for IA: Within 24hrs-acknowledge your IA behavior- repair- move towards partner not distancing)

I'm also recovering from other addiction(s): _____
_____.

My sobriety date from intentionally lying or omitting the truth to my partner is: _____.

In the last 7 days, I ____ (did/didn't) break any sobriety boundaries. If I did, they were _____and the consequences I did are ____

I _____ do/don't have a 24 tell policy and I ____ did/didn't have to use it this week

_____ is the day each week I do my Couples Accountability meeting and ___I did/didn't do it in the last 7 days

The last Workgroup meeting I attended was: _____   I attended _____ other 12 step sexual addiction meeting(s) in the last 7 days.

I did my Morning RECOVERY prayers ____ out of 7 days and I did my Evening RECOVERY prayers ____ out of 7 days

_____
_____
_____

   I made Calls ____ out of the last 7 days; I talked to someone ____ times in the last 7 days and did __ pushups for days I didn't call

I'm on step ____ in my *SA* Steps workbook; I completed ____ pages in the last 7 days and I'm on page ____; Last worked on it ____

_____
_____

I'm on step ____ in my *IA* or *MA* Steps workbook; I completed ____ pages in the last 7 days and I'm on page ____; Last worked on it ____

_____
_____

My workgroup step partner is _____ and I've scheduled with him to share my next step on _____ (date)

_____
_____

In the last 7 days, In my 101 Freedom Exercises workbook, I did exercises ____; In my IA exercise work book, I did exercises ____

IF IA

- I did the 3-Dailies ____ out of the last 7 days

- I did connection exercises with my partner ____ out of the last 7 days

- The day each week I do my date with my partner is _____ and I _____ did/didn't do it in the last 7 days

- I _____ do/don't have a Sexual agreement plan with my partner and I _____ did/didn't follow it in the last 7 days

- I _____ did/didn't have to do consequences in the last 7 days. If I did, those were_____

I did/didn't play the victim towards my partner in the last 7 days   If I did, I did it by: _____
_____

I did/didn't *half measure* it in my recovery in the last 7 days If I did, I did it by: _____

I'm going to strengthen my recovery in the next 7 days by:
_____

We have been told that by many couples that this check-in sheet is useful while they are trying to establish consistency within recovery. For the wounding partner, it serves as a reminder of the items they should be paying attention to. For the wounded partner, it gives them a picture of some of the many things the wounding partner is working on. We recommend that a weekly day and time be set aside for the wounding partner to go through the items on their check-in sheet with the wounded partner. We also recommend that the wounding partner ask the wounded partner to give them feedback on areas of recovery that could use improvement.

Item #4: 24-hour tell policy

To build trust, we recommend that the wounding partner agree to a 24-hour tell policy. By this, we mean that the wounding partner will notify the wounded partner of any sexually acting out behavior, gaslighting, manipulating, or lying within 24 hours of that failure. Additionally, the wounding partner needs to inform the wounded partner what consequence(s) they did in conjunction with the failure. If the wounding partner has not yet done a consequence, they should inform the wounded partner what the consequence will be and when they are going to do it within the next 24 hours.

We most often recommend the 24-hour tell policy for those who are struggling with sexual or pornography addiction and intimacy avoidance. If you are a wounding partner reading this, we understand that you might be apprehensive about telling your partner about your failures when it comes to your recovery plan. However, in our experience, your partner is much more likely to have an issue with your deception around your behavior than they are about the behavior itself. (Of course, the caveat here is that that the behavior wasn't associated with a dealbreaker such as having another sexual affair). Time and time again, wounded partners tell us that the lies told by to them by the wounding partner are even harder to get over than the behavior itself. Adherence to the 24-hour tell policy will help with the issue of deception.

Item #5: Recovery deep dive

While it is important that the wounding partner regret their behavior, tell the wounded partner they are sorry, and promise to never do it again, it is rarely enough to create true safety and consistency in the relationship. This is because the wounding partner's decision to engage in infidelity-related behavior is often tied to past trauma and core beliefs. These thing must be dealt with on a deep level if the wounding partner is to overcome the need to engage in infidelity-related behavior in the future. If you are a wounding partner reading this, we would encourage you to engage in counseling or coaching to discover the attitudes and beliefs that led up to your infidelity-related behavior.

Item #6: Trust-building with micro-trusts

Trust building, of course, applies to the larger issue of infidelity-related behaviors and related recovery plans that entail meetings, counseling, etc. However, the term "micro-trusts" applies to the seemingly small or unrelated things that wounding partners do every day. Wounded partners tell us time and time again that they consistently watch their partner's behavior to see if they are exhibiting any areas where they can't be trusted. This can include things that are seemingly unrelated to infidelity such as taking the garbage out as promised and without a bad attitude, helping with the kids, paying the bills on time, and being where the wounding partner said they were going to be. We refer to these areas of trust as micro-trusts. The reason these areas of micro-trust are such a big deal to wounded partners is that they are looking for evidence of a commitment to change on the wounding partner's part.

If you are a wounding partner, don't tell yourself that inconsistencies, however small, won't matter to your wounded partner. They will. We need you to understand that your partner will likely be examining your everyday behavior for signs that you are not to be trusted. If you can at all help it, we would encourage you not to give them a reason to feel that you are continuing to lie to them. Although some of your behavior may seem inconsequential to you, inconsistencies between your words and behavior will likely trigger your partner. Some examples of this could be telling them that you are going to be at a certain location for a meeting and not notifying them if the venue changes, telling them you are going out with a certain group of people and not letting them know that people have been added to your party, or telling them you are going to a particular restaurant and then going to another without letting them know. These could all be construed as an inability on your part to take the breach of trust you have created in the relationship seriously. Although the scenarios we have listed are relatively obvious as to why they could worry a wounded partner, we would like to point out that there will likely be other seemingly unrelated areas where not showing consistency could bother your partner as well. Some common ones include helping with the household without complaint, following through on agreements regarding childcare/child rearing, and doing the bare minimum instead of the effort required to do something well.

PART 23

Relationship Consistency

Now that we have covered the important areas where wounding partners need to be consistent, we would like to cover two areas in which both parties need to be consistent if the rebuilding of trust is to become a possibility.

Item #1: Engaging in recovery-focused activities

Recovery from betrayal is often an isolating process since many couples struggling with issues common to it don't feel comfortable sharing their struggles with friends and family. This is why it is imperative that both the wounding and wounded partners engage in recovery-focused activities such as attending groups, classes, intensives, seminars, and individual coaching or counseling. We would especially like to emphasize the importance of group activities—both as a couple and as individuals. At Becoming Well, we offer work groups, seminars, and individual or group intensives as a way of supporting our clients through the process. We are told on a regular basis that group recovery activities help them feel less isolated, maintain a sense of hopefulness, and learn strategies from others that help them manage their own situations. For wounded partners in particular, group recovery activities help ease their emotional burdens by having a place to vent where they will be understood. They also have reported making important connections with other individuals that help them feel supported outside of group activities. For wounding partners, group recovery can provide much-needed accountability, a non-judgmental place to work on issues, as well as insight as to what has worked for others struggling with similar issues.

Item #2: Adherence to the communication plan

If you will remember, we discussed a 3-part communication plan in the safety section of this book. The three parts consist of general ground-rules for communication, the trigger plan, and the time-out protocol. Since we previously, covered these thoroughly we will not take the time here to cover the details again. Instead, we would like to stress how important it is that both the wounding and the wounded partner adhere to all three parts of the communication plan consistently. Betrayal creates stress and pressure in a relationship unlike anything else. As a result, communication around infidelity-related issues can cause severe communication break downs that often result in one or both partners throwing in the towel.

Although we often work with couples that were experiencing major breakdowns in communication prior to the discovery or disclosure of infidelity, we also work with a fair percentage of them that claim to have had very few communication issues prior. Whatever the case, betrayal can, in and of itself, create a situation in which communication breakdowns happen frequently, especially in the beginning. As previously mentioned, some of the most common culprits we see in our office of communication stall-outs are:

- Name-calling or other insults
- Character assassination
- Defending or blame-shifting
- Threatening

- Stonewalling

- Non-verbal signs of disrespect such as eye-rolling or heavy sighing

- Mind-reading

- "Always" and "never" statements

When it comes to rebuilding trust in order to save a relationship, it is important for both parties to remember that the other is not the enemy. Instead, it is imperative that both the wounded and wounding partners give up the idea of winning an argument. When individuals in a relationship communicate in order to win, the relationship loses. This is especially hard for the wounded partner to remember since the wounding partner seems exactly like an enemy in their own camp. However, if you hope to save your relationship, you must communicate in a respectful way. Although it can be tempting to take shots at your partner for hurting or humiliating you, a failure by either party to adhere to the communication plan is like being out in the middle of the ocean and shooting holes in your own boat. The relationship has a high likelihood of eventually sinking beyond retrieval. This is not to say that anger and other strong emotions cannot be expressed. They can and should. However, it is important that they are expressed in a way that nurtures the relationship instead of destroying it. Adhering to the 3-part communication plan will help you accomplish this.

Wounded Partner Consistency

Aside from adhering to the communication plan, the area that we most commonly see the wounded partner lack consistency in is requiring the wounding partner to be ongoingly accountable for their behavior. This is not to say that the wounded partner should micro-manage the wounding partner's recovery. However, we find in a number of couples that the wounded partner is so eager to move on from the pain caused by the betrayal that they move away from requiring ongoing accountability from the wounding partner because doing so reminds them of that pain. Although we can certainly understand why this would be the case, we almost always see this backfire. Although there is certainly a time when couples decided not to talk about the infidelity on a regular basis, dropping the requirement for the wounding partner to be ongoingly accountable early on in recovery is typically a decision made from an unhealthy place of wishing to stay in denial about the reality of the situation.

Although a requirement for ongoing accountability in a relationship should never be used to punish a wounding partner, it is a fundamental part of any romantic relationship. While each partner should be accountable to the other, it is especially important to the rebuilding trust process that the wounding partner is ongoingly accountable. Infidelity shows a profound lack of self-awareness as well as a lack of empathy and awareness of how the wounding partner's behavior affects their partner. A commitment to ongoing accountability will help the wounding partner build self-awareness, build empathy, and collaborate with the wounded partner on how they can help ensure the success of the relationship moving forward by doing the things that show commitment.

Patience is Key

When it comes to rebuilding trust, patience is key. This is especially true for the wounding partner. Every day in our offices, we hear wounding partners make comments such as, "when are they going to get over this?" and "I've done all I can do to say I'm sorry, I don't understand why they can't let this go." Rebuilding trust takes a long time, and so does forgiveness. Asking a wounded partner to "get over it" before they are ready conveys disrespect for their feelings and demanding they forgive within a timeframe specified by the wounding partner conveys selfishness on the wounding partner's part.

One of the areas that seems to be the hardest for wounding partners to have patience is in the questioning phase of recovery. It is not uncommon for the wounded partner to ask multiple questions (and even the same question repeatedly) daily for the first 3-6 months following the discovery or disclosure of any type of betrayal. This holds especially true for sexual and emotional infidelity. **We want to stress that this is a completely normal phase of recovery.** If you are a wounding partner reading this, we would encourage you to accept this as a part of recovery and commit to answering your partner's questions as thoroughly and as patiently as possible. **If you answer begrudgingly, get defensive, refuse to answer, or complain that they are repeatedly asking you to answer what seems like the same question over and over, you will, at best, prolong the process and, at worst, put your relationship in further jeopardy.**

Another area where patience is often required is within the communication plan. This is especially true if a couple has had a hard time with communication prior to the betrayal. When this is case, healthy communication often takes time and patience to establish. It is unfortunate that good communication must be established under the stressful circumstances that betrayal creates, but such is the reality of the situation. Even if a couple's communication seemed relatively healthy prior to the betrayal, the intense pain and stress that follows is enough to send a couple's communication way off course.

In his book *The Seven Principles of Making Marriage Work*, authors John Gottman and Nan Silver describe what they term as the "Four Horseman of the Apocalypse". These "four horsemen" are:

- Criticism
- Contempt
- Defensiveness
- Stonewalling

The reason the authors call these the Four Horseman of the Apocalypse is that, when they are present for an extended period of time, they tend to predict the death of a relationship. The first Horseman, criticism, is different than presenting a complaint. Bringing a specific issue to your partner's attention is acceptable. However, if it is accompanied by an attack on your partner's character, it is considered to be criticism and will often result in your partner becoming defensive. The second Horseman, contempt, happens when one partner takes a position of superiority over the other. Contempt is typically conveyed through things like sarcasm, ridiculing with words or mimicry, eye rolling or other disrespectful body language, and name calling. The third Horseman, defensiveness, is typically a response to criticism or perceived criticism. We very commonly see defensiveness in IA relationships. Defensiveness is often displayed through playing the victim, reversing accusations (I know I did "x", but you did it too), blame (I wouldn't have done "x" if you didn't do "y"), and excuse-making. The fourth Horseman, stonewalling, can also be a response to criticism but it also a common response to contempt. It is also present in many IA relationships when the IA refuses to admit to wrongdoing because they want to retain power and control. It can also come out when either partner becomes flooded with emotion. Stonewalling often looks like giving up, saying comments such as, "never mind" or "fine" and following those comments with silence. Stonewalling can also look like the silent treatment or prolonged periods of no talking.

When we work with couples, it is not uncommon for us to see most, if not all, of the Four Horseman show up. Early on in recovery, helping couples eradicate them often becomes top priority. It is important for you to understand that the presence of the Four Horseman of the Apocalypse does not spell certain doom for your relationship and is even a normal occurrence after betrayal. However, prolonged use of any of these tactics will result in damage separate from that done by betrayal that could lead to the relationship's end. Luckily, John Gottman's research has proven that there are antidotes to each of the Horseman. These are:

- Gentle Start Up
- Building a Culture of Appreciation
- Taking Responsibility
- Psychological Self-Soothing

Antidote number one, the gentle start up, should be used to counteract criticism. This looks like honestly expressing feelings using "I" statements. The Speaker-Listener technique we mentioned previously is great for this. Antidote number two, building a culture of appreciation, should be used to counteract contempt. Building a culture of appreciation looks like reminding yourself of your partner's positive attributes and expressing gratitude for the good things they have done. If you refer back to Step 5 of the time-out protocol, you will notice that we ask each partner to state at least one thing that they appreciate about the other. This, along with other tools you will find in the final section on intimacy, will begin building a culture of appreciation in your relationship. The third antidote, taking responsibility, should be used to counteract defensiveness. Taking responsibility includes apologizing for wrongdoing and validating where your partner is coming from, even if you don't agree. We have discussed taking responsibility multiple times throughout these chapters. The fourth antidote, psychological self-soothing, should be used to counteract stonewalling. Instead of stonewalling your partner when you become emotionally overwhelmed, or yelling at them, use the Time-Out Protocol described earlier in this book to calm your emotions down. It is important to note that each partner should give the other a set time when they plan on coming back to the conversation in order to avoid abandoning their partner in the midst of their pain.

We are all human. As such, it is expected that failures in communication, and even the Four Horseman, will come up. When these inevitable failures do occur, it is important that each partner take immediate responsibility for their own actions. Although a failure to remain consistent with any part of the plan is not ideal, most (if not all) people understand that humans make mistakes and are willing to accept an apology in order to move on. When either partner admits to having failed with some part of the recovery plan, this will also build trust. If either one makes a mistake and refuses to admit it, even when called to account for it, it will break down trust in the relationship even further. The same holds true for a situation in which either partner defends themselves regarding their failure. Remember, defensiveness is one of the Four Horseman of the Apocalypse.

PART 24

Rebuilding Trust Pyramid Layer #4

Intimacy

Intimacy is something that we all crave, and yet so many of us avoid it. To have true intimacy in our primary relationship, we must be willing to expose our innermost selves to one another. This is something many people refuse to do. This is especially true in intimacy avoidant relationships, where intimacy is avoided by the IA at all costs. To be truly intimate with our partner, we must be willing to share every aspect of ourselves. We must be willing to let the other person see us—flaws and all. Intimacy involves consistently sharing our true selves with our partner in an unconstrained way without fear of rejection.

When people talk about intimacy, they most commonly refer to sex. While sex can be an expression of intimacy, it is not true intimacy in and of itself. A large percentage of our clients who have engaged in infidelity-related behavior are actually searching for intimacy and, instead, using sex as a replacement for it. Sex, in and of itself, often requires no true intimacy at all. Aside from the risk of possibly being rejected for actually getting to have sex, the act of sex takes very little risk on our part. This is why sex outside of the primary relationship, empty sex within the primary relationship (checking out emotionally), pornography, and even emotional affairs become enticing temporary substitutes for real intimacy to someone who struggles to share their true self with their partner. In the case of addiction, these temporary substitutes are clear examples of ways in which a person struggling to participate in true intimacy begins to fill the void in destructive ways.

Types of Intimacy

When it comes to intimacy, there are 5 different areas that we typically talk about. These are:

- Physical. This includes anything from small displays of affection such as placing a hand on someone's leg to large displays of affection such as sex.

- Emotional. This means feeling emotionally connected with your partner through the safe sharing of emotions and thoughts.

- Spiritual. This involves being able to share your spirituality with your partner without fear of judgement.

- Intellectual. This involves being able to share your thoughts and opinions with each other in a safe environment. It also involves stimulating each other's minds.

- Experiential. This type of intimacy describes the bonding that can happen through shared activity.

People experience intimacy in these areas at different levels, depending on who they are interacting with. Regarding healthy committed, romantic relationships, healthy intimacy should be shared at several levels. This includes being able to share your thoughts and opinions, hopes and dreams, feelings, vulnerabilities, and needs.

When betrayal happens in a relationship, it undermines all areas of intimacy—not just physical. This is because there is a lack of safety in the relationship, especially for the wounded partner. For them, the feeling of safety they may have had that rested on the sense that they were working toward something with a partner that was equally committed to the health of the relationship has been completely undermined. If you are a wounding partner reading this, we would stress the importance of understanding this truth.

When it comes to intimacy after betrayal, aside from the wounding partner ending their infidelity-related behavior, the expression of remorse, empathy, and compassion are the most important components of rekindling closeness. If the wounding partner cannot express remorse for what they have done, and show empathy and compassion toward their partner, intimacy is unlikely to develop, and recovery will stall out. When we think about real love, we tend to think about emotions and behaviors that are characterized by commitment and self-sacrifice. In committed relationships, this means laying down personal plans and agendas that conflict with the good of the relationship. Infidelity is the antithesis of love because it involves self-focus to the detriment of the relationship and the wounded partner. If intimacy is to be restored, love must be shown by the wounding partner's actions and attitudes. These actions and attitudes must support the good of the relationship and must show that the wounding partner is no longer putting their wishes and desires above those of the wounded partner. This includes defending, blaming, minimization, stonewalling, and any other attitude or action that puts the wounding partner's need to be right or protected from shame above the good of the wounded partner and the relationship.

Conversely, if intimacy is to be restored, the wounded partner will need to find a way to work through the resentments caused by the wounding partner's betrayal. Additionally, strict adherence to the communication plan will show a commitment on the wounded partner's part to the good of the relationship. Yelling, shaming, name-calling, although typical after a betrayal of trust, will hinder intimacy because the wounded partner is focused on their own need to vent rather than on the good of the relationship. When we make this statement to wounded partners, they often counter with the fact that they should not have to worry about the good of the relationship when the wounding partner obviously didn't care about it. While we certainly understand this sentiment, we must point out that two wrongs do not make a right. Each person in the relationship must take responsibility for their own actions, regardless of what the other person has done in the past or is still doing.

Resuming Sex After Betrayal

Probably the most common questions we get from couples we work with surround resuming sex after betrayal. First, we would like to state that when to resume sex after betrayal is a personal decision that must be made by the individuals in the relationship. That being said, we usually recommend a hiatus from sex within the first 60-90 days after disclosure of sexual infidelity because sex after infidelity is complicated and the first 2-3 months are typically fraught with indecisiveness and emotional volatility. Resuming sex too soon can cause confusion, not to mention that sex, when used incorrectly, can cover up a multitude of issues related to intimacy that need to be focused on.

Although most of the couples we work with have trouble resuming sex after infidelity, we felt it important to mention that a significant percentage of them actually report sex being more frequent and better than ever. This is not uncommon and is usually fueled by the insecurity created by the betrayal—which then creates an intense need to reconnect. It can also be fueled by the wounded partner's need to be desirable to the wounding partner. Although we want to stress that this is a completely normal response to the pain caused by betrayal, we want to also mention that it is not likely to last—and that is okay. This can be confusing for both partners, especially for the wounding partner, but it does not mean that the relationship is over or that it was wrong. There is no script for resuming sexual intimacy after infidelity. Additionally, if you want to continue to have sex on a regular basis, that is okay too. However, we would caution you not to use sex as your only form of intimacy. It is imperative that you both work on strengthening your bond in the other areas of intimacy as well. Otherwise, your relationship will likely fail to thrive in the long term.

If you are a wounded partner who has had trouble with sexual intimacy and is considering resuming sex after betrayal, we advise that you honor your mind and body while making your decision. This means paying close attention to the signs that you are experiencing any sort of trauma response. These can include feeling pressured to resume sex, tension around the subject, disassociation, intrusive thoughts, extreme anger, aggressiveness, overwhelming shame, or hyperarousal before, during, and after sex. The presence of these things are completely normal after experiencing the trauma of betrayal. However, they are signs that you may need to slow things down. Additionally, if your relationship has suffered from your partner's sexual infidelity, we always recommend STI/STD testing prior to resuming sex. You may find it helpful to work with a qualified coach or counselor on this subject, as going through this process can often produce intense emotions.

When it comes to resuming sex after betrayal, especially after sexual infidelity, communication and patience on the part of both partners are key. Resuming sexual intimacy can be a tricky business. The presence of flashbacks, intrusive thoughts, and resentments along with the erosion of trust make it difficult. Truly intimate sex requires vulnerability, and vulnerability is hard to come by when trust has been betrayed. This is why it is imperative that both partners stick to their recovery plans whenever possible. If defending, minimization, blaming, stonewalling, and unbridled emotional expression are taking place on a regular basis, sex will often feel unsafe. We feel it important to point out that resuming sexual intimacy after betrayal, especially after sexual infidelity, is usually slow going. Both partners will need to have patience with themselves as well as with the other. Making accommodations for your sex life in the light of betrayal is paramount. Unfortunately, the expectation that you can just pick up where you left off is unrealistic. If you do not realize this and make accommodations for it, you risk hurting yourself and your partner. There is no deadline for when things should be "back to normal". The truth is that your sexual intimacy may never be the same as it was prior to the betrayal. However, this does not mean that things can't ever be good again. Give yourselves time and patience while you reestablish your sexual relationship.

It is important that the wounded partner build up their vocabulary when it comes to expressing their needs around safety regarding sex. This includes not only expressing when they do and do not wish to engage in sexual intimacy, but also communication about how their sexuality has been affected by their partner's betrayal. Additionally, it is important that the couple be in regular communication regarding sex. This can be difficult to do in the face of trauma, particularly if the couple's sex life was a point of contention prior to the betrayal. We recommend that couples do not try to go this communication alone but enlist the help of a trained coach or counselor to help facilitate the process. We cannot stress enough that whoever you hire to help you should be trained and experienced in the area of recovery, as your situation will present unique obstacles and challenges that are unlike other intimacy issues found in relationships that have not been affected by betrayal.

Regarding intrusive thoughts and flashbacks, we want to stress that this is a normal part of the trauma response to betrayal. The frequency we see this in our practice can vary from person to person. However, in the case of sexual infidelity, we see at least some form of this in 100% of our clients. It is important that the couple communicate about this on a regular basis and that the wounding partner show empathy and concern for the wounded partner's experience. It is also important to understand that when the wounded partner has a traumatic response, both partners should stop the sexual activity to talk through the issue prior to resuming. We have never seen good results from wounded partners "powering through" traumatic responses. Nor have we seen benefit to the relationship or the wounded partner when the wounding partner pressures them to keep going or acts inconvenienced or annoyed that they had to stop.

If you are a wounding partner reading this, we would like to impress upon you that your partner's trauma response is involuntary and is not something they are doing to punish or shame you. Your partner's traumatic responses are a result of your infidelity-related behavior. We do not say this to shame you in any way. However, it is imperative that you understand the consequences of your behavior and show your partner compassion and empathy when they are working through their reactions.

One final thing we would like to add here is that much of the work to be done regarding triggers, intrusive thoughts, and flashbacks falls to the wounded partner. Although this may seem unfair, there is no way around it. Unfortunately, the wounding partner can only do so much to help the wounded partner heal. Working through resentments, developing productive communication skills, and finding ways to self-soothe when triggered are all important to the process of rebuilding sexual intimacy. Additionally, the wounded partner may also benefit significantly from EMDR therapy. Eye Movement Desensitization and Reprocessing (EMDR) therapy is a therapy that has been proven to be effective when it comes symptoms of trauma such as PTSD and has helped many betrayed partners heal. This type of therapy uses bilateral stimulation to help the brain work through the fears, thoughts, beliefs, and pain often associated with betrayal trauma.

PART 25

The Importance of Cultivating Good Intimacy Habits

As we alluded to previously, it is important that your approach to intimacy after betrayal be a balanced one. This means cultivating intimacy in all areas. When it comes to physical intimacy, it is important to note that non-sexual touch is extremely important in creating safety in the relationship. This is especially true if addiction has been a factor. If you are a wounding partner and have an addiction to sex or pornography, it will be important that you learn to express your desire for your partner in other ways besides asking for sex. Many times wounded partners in relationships with addicts report feeling used. When a wounding partner only expresses their need for intimacy in a sexual manner or only seems interested in their partner when they know that sex is on the table, this compounds the problem. It is also important to note that an addictive mindset can put undue pressure on the wounded partner to resume sex before they are truly ready. If you are a wounding partner reading this and addiction is an issue for you, you will need to pay close attention to how much pressure you are putting on the wounded partner to fill your sexual needs. Badgering, demanding sex from them as "proof" that they love you, reacting negatively with hurt, anger, sadness or resentment, or threatening negative consequences to the relationship (either overtly or subtly) is coercive. Although this may get you what you want in the short term, it will eventually backfire.

When it comes to the cultivation and development of healthy intimacy habits, it is important to realize that the process is similar to building any healthy habit. When developing habits that support an intimate relationship, here are some things to keep in mind:

- Focus on creating one habit at a time (in the case of recovery, this could be several related habits)

- Commit to a set amount of time for each habit (usually between 30 and 90 days)

- Anchor the new habit in something you already do regularly. (An example would be doing an intimacy-building exercise prior to engaging in your morning routine of getting ready for work.)

- Do the intimacy-building activity every day without fail

- Plan for challenges or obstacles by using if/then scenarios. (An example of this would be if you can't do the activity before work, then you will take time to do it in the middle of your day.)

- Put accountability in place around your new habit

Once a couple gets through the discovery/disclosure phase, it will be important that intimacy-building routines be established. The idea here is to give each partner a chance to connect to the other while giving the relationship room to breathe away from discussions around the betrayal. This often includes the following:

- Regular dates

- Meditation, gratitude and/or prayer

- Daily expression of appreciation

- Daily sharing of feelings
- Shared activities
- Discussion about the betrayal or related issues
- Sex

Let's take a closer look at each one:

Intimacy-Builder #1: Regular Dates

For couples looking to rebuild intimacy, regular time set aside to spend together is key. We recommend that dates be done on a weekly basis. One caveat here is that the time set aside for the date should not be used to discuss the betrayal. The purpose of a weekly date is to allow the couple time to reconnect outside of what has taken place. Discussions after betrayal are often all-consuming. Early on, it is not unusual for conversations around what happened to take up several hours per day. If you are to reconnect with each other in any meaningful way, it will be important to protect your weekly date by committing to each other that discussion of infidelity-related issues is off limits.

Weekly dates are particularly important for relationships in which intimacy avoidance is a complicating factor. Since these relationships are typically devoid of true intimacy, time set aside to focus on one another is part of recovery. When we work with intimacy avoidants during intensives, we always include the weekly date as part of the recovery plan. It is important to note that the IA should plan the date each week as a part of their commitment to ongoing recovery. The IA should plan the date for a set period of time. Once recovery in this area is established, each partner can trade off planning the date. For couples where intimacy avoidance is not an issue, partners can take turns in the planning.

In order to facilitate connection, we recommend that you commit to asking each other questions in order to get to know each other better and to discover what each of you appreciates about the other. John and Julie Gottman, co-authors of the book *Eight Dates: Essential Conversations for a Lifetime of Love*, have developed whole card decks with many open-ended questions that couples can ask each other in order to help facilitate connection. Generally speaking, questions should not be ones that can be answered with a simple yes or no, but ones that require thought. Here are some examples:

- If you could be one age forever, which age would you choose and why?
- What in your life makes you feel the most grateful? Why?
- What is the best gift you have ever received? Why?
- If you could live in any era, what would it be and why?
- What have you done that you feel the proudest of? Why?
- What is the funniest thing you have ever had happen to you?

Intimacy-Builder #2: Meditation, Gratitude, or Prayer

For those couples who pray, prayer is a time when partners can feel spiritually connected. It gives each partner insight into what is important to the other, which can bring a couple closer. If you are not a couple who prays, meditation is also a powerful way to spiritually connect. Additionally, making a gratitude list is not only a great practice, but it can also help partners feel closer when each one learns what the other is grateful for.

Intimacy-Builder #3: Daily Expression of Appreciation

Let's face it, few things can put a negative spin on a relationship quite like infidelity can. If you refer back to the time-out protocol in the section on safety, you will see that we ask partners to state at least one positive attribute about each other prior to resuming a tough conversation. This is because it creates a culture of appreciation in the relationship. Much in the same vein, we recommend that each partner state at least 2 things they appreciate or admire about the other one at the start of each day and at least 1 thing prior to going to bed each night. If you are not able to be together in person, consider texting or emailing each other. Please note that this does not cancel out the legitimate pain caused by the wounding partner's betrayal in any way. However, when expressing appreciation is made a priority, it can help combat the negativity that inherently comes from the discovery or disclosure of betrayal.

Intimacy-Builder #4: Daily Sharing of Feelings

Many couples have trouble sharing emotions with each other. This is particularly true of relationships characterized by intimacy avoidance. When we work with couples, we always ask them to share two feelings with each other at the same time each day. One caveat here is that the feelings shared should not be related to those caused by the betrayal. Much like weekly dates, this time should be protected from the turmoil caused by the wounding partner's behavior. We recommend that two feelings be shared at the same time as daily expression of appreciation.

Intimacy-Builder #5: Shared Activities

Shared activities are important building blocks of intimacy and friendship. These shared activities should take place at a time when you can both agree to put discussion of the betrayal aside in order to give your relationship some breathing room. Some simple ideas for shared activities include:

- Exercise together
- Reading the same book and discussing it
- Cooking a meal together
- Eating together
- Volunteering together

Intimacy-Builder #6: Discussion About the Betrayal and Related Issues

For couples dealing with the aftermath of betrayal, it is important that time is set aside to discuss the betrayal, feelings surrounding what has happened, and any other related issues. It is especially important to note that the wounding partner should make themselves available to the wounded partner as a way of showing them that they care about what has happened. When the wounding partner avoids conversations, or shuts them down with defensiveness, indifference, annoyance, or stonewalling, they send a message to the wounded partner that they don't care about how their actions have affected them. We understand that conversations around betrayal are likely uncomfortable for the wounding partner and often bring on feelings of guilt and even shame. However, some of the most powerful examples we have seen of couples who have healed from betrayal are those where the wounding partner made it a point of being available for these tough conversations by asking the wounded partner what questions they could answer or if they needed to express their feelings regarding what they had done.

Intimacy-Builder #7: Sex

As we previously explained, sex after betrayal (particularly sexual infidelity) can be tricky. (See previous section on resuming sex after betrayal.) We want to reiterate that patience, compassion, and empathy are crucial to this process. We also want to point out that it is imperative that sex be resumed when the wounded partner is ready and that it should not be driven by the wounding partner's needs to be satisfied. Many couples we work with find it helpful to schedule a time to be sexually intimate with each other. We realize that scheduling sex may seem counter-intuitive when it comes to intimacy. However, in our experience, the subject of sex is often avoided by couples—especially after betrayal. Scheduling a regular time to be sexually intimate can provide opportunities for a couple to work through the many issues that inevitably arise from betrayal.

Conclusion

As we stated in the introduction, our goal in writing this book was to give you a clear path to rebuilding trust after betrayal. We feel that the Rebuilding Trust Pyramid provides that clear path. Hopefully you do as well. The four layers of honesty, safety, consistency, and intimacy—along with the information contained here regarding the components of each of these—should provide you with what you need in order to begin your healing journey.

When it comes to the bottom layer, honesty, you discovered that honesty is the foundation of every relationship. This foundation has been severely damaged by the wounding partner's choices. As a result, it is imperative that honesty moving forward is given great emphasis, as it is pivotal to the rebuilding trust process. Until honesty is established, recovery will stall out. Next, you learned several ways in which you can begin to build safety back into your relationship. As we explained, betrayal violates the safety of the relationship and it is essential that each partner, especially the wounding partner, do their part to see that safety is restored. Next, you learned about how to create consistency as a part of cementing safety in your relationship. Although this layer of rebuilding trust can take the longest to establish, a couple is likely to continue to struggle to rebuild trust if much time and effort is not put toward strengthening this layer. Lastly, you learned how honesty, safety, and consistency are all ingredients to rebuilding intimacy in the relationship. Without these key ingredients, partners will fail to build true intimacy with each other. Additionally, we provided you with some ideas on how to begin to connect with each other in small but meaningful ways in order to help strengthen your bond.

At Becoming Well, we work with couples and individuals to help restore relationships after betrayal. We also work with couples whose relationships are suffering from the devastating effects of intimacy avoidance. If you are interested in our various workgroups, classes, sessions, and intensives, please visit us at www.mybecomingwell.com to learn more about what we offer.

Finally, we would like to thank you for taking the time to read this book. We know that you and your relationship will benefit greatly from following the advice contained here. As always, we wish you all the best in your journey to recovery.

References

Bower, S., Bower, G. (2004) *Asserting Yourself: A Practical Guide for Positive Change*. Addison-Wesley Pub. Co. Reading, MA

Chapman, G., Thomas, J. (2022) *The 5 Apology Languages: The Secret to Healthy Relationships*. Northfield Publishing. Chicago, IL.

Cluff-Schade, L., Sandberg, J. (2012) Healing the Attachment Injury of Marital Infidelity Using Emotionally Focused Couples Therapy: A Case Illustration. The American Journal of Family Therapy. 40(5), p. 435

Contributors to the Converus Website, https://converus.com/

Dweck, C. (2014) "Developing a Growth Mindset with Carol Dweck", TED Talks, https://www.youtube.com/watch?v=hiiEeMN7vbQ

Dweck, C. Ph. D. (2006) *Mindset: The New Psychology of Success*. Random House Publishing. New York City, NY

Folkman, J. (2019, 17 October) "Your Inconsistency is More Noticeable Than You Think", Forbes. https://www.forbes.com/sites/joefolkman/2019/10/17/your-inconsistency-is-more-noticeable-than-you-think/?sh=558938e13d50

Gordon, K. C., & Baucom, D. H. (1999). A multitheoretical intervention for promoting recovery from extramarital affairs.

Clinical Psychology: Science and

Practice, 6(4), 382–399. https://doi.org/10.1093/clipsy.6.4.382

Gottman, J., Schwartz-Gottman, J. Abrams, D., Abrams, R. *Eight Dates: Essential Conversations for a Lifetime of Love.* Workman Publishing Company, Inc. New York City, NY

Gottman, J., Silver, N. (2000). *The Seven Principals for Making Marriage Work.* Orion Publishing Group. London, England.

Guha, A. (2021) "When it Might Not Be Gaslighting". Psychology Today. https://www.psychologytoday.com/us/blog/prisons-and-pathos/202107/when-it-might-not-be-gaslighting

Harvard Health, (2020, 6 July), "Understanding the Stress Response", https://www.health.harvard.edu/staying-healthy/understanding-the-stress-response#:~:text=The%20sympathetic%20nervous%20system%20functions,system%20acts%20like%20a%20brake.

Iacono WG, Ben-Shakhar G. Current status of forensic lie detection with the comparison question technique: An update of the 2003 National Academy of Sciences report on polygraph testing. Law Hum Behav. 2019 Feb;43(1):86-98. doi: 10.1037/lhb0000307. Epub 2018 Oct 4. PMID: 30284848.

Johnson, S. M. (2004). Attachment Theory: A Guide for Healing Couple Relationships. In W. S. Rholes & J. A. Simpson (Eds.), Adult attachment: Theory, research, and clinical implications (pp. 367–387). Guilford Publications.

Marin, R., Christensen, A., Atkins, D., (2014), Infidelity and

Behavioral Couple Therapy: Relationship Outcomes Over 5 Years Following Therapy. American Psychological Association. Couple and Family Psychology Research and Practice. 3(1), 1-12

Perel, E. (2014) "Are We Asking Too Much of Our Spouses?", TED Radio Hour, https://www.npr.org/transcripts/301825600

Perry SL, Schleifer C. Till Porn Do Us Part? A Longitudinal Examination of Pornography Use and Divorce. J Sex Res. 2018 Mar-Apr;55(3):284-296. doi: 10.1080/00224499.2017.1317709. Epub 2017 May 12. PMID: 28497988.

Pittman, F. (1990) *Private Lies: Infidelity and the Betrayal of Intimacy*. Norton. New York

Real, T. (2008) *The New Rules of Marriage: What You Need to Know to Make Love Work*. Ballantine Books. New York City, NY

Savulescu, J., Sandberg, A. (2008), Neuroenhancement of Love and Marriage: The Chemicals Between Us. Neuroethics. 1: 31-44 Doi 10.1007/s12152-007-9002-4

Tennov, D. (1989), *Love and Limerence: The Experience of Being in Love*. Scarborough House. Chelsea, MI

University Of California - Los Angeles. (2003, October 10). Rejection Really Hurts, UCLA Psychologists Find. ScienceDaily. Retrieved from www.sciencedaily.com/releases/2003/10/031010074045.htm

Vaughn, P. (2010) *Help for Therapists (and Their Clients) in Dealing With Affairs*. p. 3, Dialog Press. San Diego, CA.

Voon V, Mole TB, Banca P, Porter L, Morris L, Mitchell S, et al. (2014) Neural Correlates of Sexual Cue Reactivity in Individuals with and without Compulsive Sexual Behaviours. PLoS ONE 9(7): e102419. https://doi.org/10.1371/journal.pone.0102419

Weaver, Jane (2017, April 16) "Many cheat for a thrill, more stay for true love". Health News. https://www.nbcnews.com/health/health-news/many-cheat-thrill-more-stay-true-love-flna1c9446137

Weir, K. (2011) "The Exercise Effect", American Psychological Association, 42(11), p. 48, https://www.apa.org/monitor/2011/12/exercise

Weiss, Douglas Ph.D., (2010) *Intimacy Anorexia: Healing the Hidden Addiction in Your Marriage*, Discovery Press. Colorado Springs, CO.

Whitcomb, L. (2021, 10 May) "Why Does 'Emotional Pain' Hurt?". LiveScience. https://www.livescience.com/why-emotional-pain-hurts.html

Truth About Deception (2022), The Cheating Spouse Quiz Results, https://www.truthaboutdeception.com/community-features/online-quizzes/cheating-spouse-results.html

Young L J. The Neural Basis of Pair Bonding in a Monogamous Species: A Model for Understanding the Biological Basis of Human Behavior. In: National Research Council (US) Panel for the Workshop on the Biodemography of Fertility and Family Behavior; Wachter KW, Bulatao RA, editors. Offspring: Human Fertility Behavior in Biodemographic Perspective. Washington (DC): National Academies Press (US); 2003. 4. Available from: https://www.ncbi.nlm.nih.gov/books/NBK97287/

Glossary

24-Hour Tell Policy: An agreement between partners that if either one engages in off-limits behaviors, they will tell the other partner within 24 hours. Typically done in conjunction with a self-imposed consequence.

Ambivalence: The state of having mixed feelings or contradictory ideas about someone or something. (Oxford Languages) Ambivalence after infidelity is common for both the wounded partner and the wounding partner.

Betrayal Trauma: A type of emotional trauma that happens when a person or people that someone depends on significantly violate that person's trust or well-being. Betrayal trauma also happens when there is a severe violation of attachment.

Circle of Safety: This term is used in conjunction with therapeutic disclosure. The wounded partner's circle of safety includes friends, family members, co-workers, and any property owned or regularly visited by the wounded partner such as homes, cars, vacation rentals, etc.

Disclosure: A process in which the wounding partner willingly admits to infidelity, hidden porn usage, or any other infidelity-related behavior. Disclosure is recommended and is the most conducive to the rebuilding of trust.

Discovery: The process in which the wounding partner's infidelity-related behavior is discovered by the wounded partner accidentally or against the will of the wounding partner. Not recommended and makes the process of rebuilding trust extremely difficult.

Dribbling Disclosure: A process in which the wounded partner is given a partial information regarding their partner's infidelity-related behavior. The wounding partner, for fear of consequences, purposely holds back important information but then "dribbles" it out over time. Not recommended. The results are similar to those of discovery.

Emotional Flooding: Becoming overwhelmed with emotion to the extent that a person shuts down, screams and yells, threatens, or cries uncontrollably. Emotional flooding is a sign that the sympathetic nervous system has been engaged.

Emotional Infidelity: Also referred to as an "emotional affair". Emotional Infidelity can be defined as a situation in which a person shares an intimate, emotional connection with someone other than their partner. It is different than a platonic friendship in that it usually involves some sort of romantic or sexual tension. It also involves focusing the emotional energy that should belong to a partner on someone else.

Fight or Flight Response: A physiological reaction associated with survival that prepares the body to stay and fight or run from a situation.

Gaslighting: This term describes a subtle or overt form of manipulation in which the person doing the gaslighting attempts to sow seeds of doubt in their partner's mind about the validity of their emotions and reality.

Grooming: A form of manipulation in which the person doing the grooming builds an emotional connection or rapport with another person that appears to be genuine. The motive underneath grooming behavior can be anything from control to sex but is marked by the groomer's desire to have a particular need met, despite what it may cost the other person.

HOVA: This acronym stands for "Hand, Oral, Vaginal, Anal", and is used to describe sex acts. It is most often used in disclosure and polygraph tests because the meaning of the word "sex" can vary from person to person.

Infatuation: An intense passion for someone that is typically short-lived.

Infidelity-Related Behavior: Behavior associated with a breach of trust, disloyalty, or wrongdoing. This includes even seemingly mild behavior such as ogling or "rubbernecking".

Infidelity through Pornography: (See description for pornography) Although defining pornography use as infidelity can be controversial, we at Becoming Well hold that it is. This holds especially true if the partner using the pornography lies about it or covers it up in any way.

Intimacy Anorexia®: This term, coined by Dr. Doug Weiss, is defined as "the active and intentional withholding of emotional, physical sexual, and/or spiritual connection from a partner for the purpose of creating distance."

Intimacy Avoidance: The term intimacy avoidance refers to a situation in which one partner is withholding themselves in multiple ways from their partner. Intimacy avoidance often goes unnoticed by the person withholding themselves yet can have lasting and devastating effects on their loved ones.

Limerence: A strong state of emotional infatuation, longing, and even obsession that lasts as little as 6 months and as long as 3 years. (In some cases, longer) It is characterized by a fixation on an object—usually a particular person and the idea of that person

Limerent Object: The subject of a romantic fixation or ideal. The wounding partner will tend to exaggerate the limerent object's positive traits while simultaneously minimizing their flaws.

Lust: A very strong sexual desire

Marathon Conversation: A conversation that should take 45 minutes or less to discuss but ends up turning into a conversation that lasts for hours, and even days.

Masturbation: The stimulation of one's own genitals for the purpose of sexual arousal, sexual pleasure, or orgasm.

Micro-Trust: Considered the "baby steps" of rebuilding trust. We define micro-trusts as small areas where trust can be earned. Sometimes seemingly small breaches of trust can add up to a large problem. This is especially true when infidelity has affected a relationship.

Narcissistic Behavior: Behavior that can be characterized as arrogant, abusive, entitled, manipulative, self-serving, or egocentric. People struggling with this issue will often have an exaggerated sense of self-importance, show a lack of empathy, be highly sensitive to criticism (real or perceived), and will often use gaslighting and blame shifting as a way to escape accountability for their actions.

Pink Clouding: A term used to describe a situation in early recovery, especially from addiction and/or intimacy avoidance, where the wounding partner feels extremely optimistic about the recovery process.

Pornography: Any type of printed or visual material, whether explicit or not, that is being used for the purpose of stimulating sexual or erotic feelings and/or is used for the purpose of sexual fantasy or masturbation.

Recovery: Regaining something that was lost or damaged by engaging in certain actions or processes.

Sexual Anorexia: A condition marked by the fear, dread, or avoidance of sexual activity. Although it can be marked by impotence or other physical problems, the cause is typically psychological.

Sexual Establishment: This term includes establishments that provide live visuals for the purpose of sexual stimulation such as strip clubs, adult bookstores, peep shows, and live sex shows. It can also include bikini baristas and "breastaurants" such as Hooters and Twin Peaks.

Sexual Infidelity: Commonly referred to as "cheating". This term is used to describe a situation in which someone engages in a sexual act (HOVA) with a person who is not their spouse or committed partner.

Sympathetic Nervous System: The network of nerves that are responsible for the "fight or flight" response.

Therapeutic Disclosure: A planned and professionally facilitated event in which the wounding partner discloses to the wounded partner all of the information regarding infidelity-related behavior and/or sexual/pornography addiction.

Trigger: Any situation, idea, or action that causes intense emotions and/or emotional discomfort. In the case of infidelity, triggers are associated with traumatic events, especially the discovery of betrayal. A trauma trigger can be described as anything that reminds a person of a past trauma.

Trust: As it pertains to relationships, we define trust as the ability to feel that one's partner is a source of security, support, safety, and dependability.

Wounded Partner: A party associated with a committed relationship who has been betrayed and hurt by their relationship partner.

Wounding Partner: A party associated with a committed relationship who has committed an act of betrayal, a breach of trust, an act of wrongdoing, or an act of disloyalty that emotionally, physically, financially, and/or spiritually affects their relationship partner.

About the Authors

Matt Burton

Matt Burton is a certified sexual addiction recovery coach (SRC), partners recovery coach (PRC), partner betrayal trauma coach (PBTC), intimacy anorexia® coach (IAC) through the American Association for Sexual Addiction Therapy (AASAT). He is also a nationally certified recovery coach (NCRC), nationally certified family recovery coach (NCFRC), life coach, certified clinical trauma specialist for both individuals and families (CCTSI) (CCTSF) and certified clinical trauma specialist for trauma and addiction (CCTSA).

Matt was part of starting Pure Desire (formerly known as For Men Only/For Women Only) for pornography and sexual addiction recovery. Since 1994, Matt has worked with couples impacted by sex and pornography addiction, physical and emotional infidelity, and intimacy avoidance to help them find healing, maintain sobriety, and heal and restore their relationships.

Additionally, for over two decades, Matt has worked with men that have experienced many forms of trauma and is the author of the groundbreaking book *The Unbound Man*. He has helped men and their partners heal from trauma.

Laura Burton

Laura Burton is a trained and certified partners recovery coach (PRC), partner betrayal trauma coach (PBTC), sexual addiction recovery coach (SRC), and intimacy anorexia® coach (IAC) through the American Association for Sexual Addiction Therapy (AASAT). She is also a nationally certified life coach (NCLC) through The Addictions Academy. What makes Laura such an amazing coach and guide for partners is her own personal journey as a partner through the impacts of pornography addiction, infidelity, and intimacy avoidance.

Partners are often overlooked. Laura's ability to walk through the healing process as a partner, find profound healing and health, learn to be a part of a healthy marriage, and then turn around and help others to do the same is invaluable. She understands how living with an addict can negatively impact partners in all areas of their lives. She has helped hundreds of partners of sex addicts, unfaithful partners, and intimacy avoidants become more balanced in mind, soul, and body.

Together, Matt and Laura are co-founders of Becoming Well, LLC. They have also been instrumental in starting Intimacy ICU; a non-profit offering conferences around the United States on the subjects of rebuilding trust and intimacy, sexual addiction, sexual anorexia, intimacy avoidance, and infidelity. Additionally, Intimacy ICU offers scholarships to help couples and individuals afford the care they need while struggling to recover.

www.ingramcontent.com/pod-product-compliance
Lightning Source LLC
LaVergne TN
LVHW041758060526
838201LV00046B/1039